COVERLETS AND THE SPIRIT OF AMERICA

The Shein Coverlets

Melinda Zongor, Curator

Schiffer Publishing Ltd
4880 Lower Valley Road, Atglen, PA 19310 USA

Dedication

To my wife, Janet, whose love, advice, enthusiasm, and patience made this book possible.

Library of Congress Cataloging-in-Publication Data

Coverlets and the spirit of America: the Shein coverlets/Melinda Zongor, curator.
p. cm.
ISBN 0-7643-1660-5
1. Coverlets--United States--Catalogs. 2. Shein, Joseph--Art collections--Catalogs. 3. Shein, Janet--Art collections--Catalogs. 4. Coverlets--Private collections--United States--Catalogs. I. Zongor, Melinda.
NK9112 .C653 2002
746.9'7'0973075-dc21
2002002547

Designed by "Sue"
Type set in Americana BT/Dutch801 BT

ISBN: 0-7643-1660-5
Printed in China

Published by Schiffer Publishing Ltd.
4880 Lower Valley Road
Atglen, PA 19310
Phone: (610) 593-1777; Fax: (610) 593-2002
E-mail: Schifferbk@aol.com
Please visit our web site catalog at **www.schifferbooks.com**
We are always looking for people to write books on new and related subjects. If you have an idea for a book please contact us at the above address.

This book may be purchased from the publisher.
Include $3.95 for shipping.
Please try your bookstore first.
You may write for a free catalog.

In Europe, Schiffer books are distributed by
Bushwood Books
6 Marksbury Ave.
Kew Gardens
Surrey TW9 4JF England
Phone: 44 (0) 20 8392-8585; Fax: 44 (0) 20 8392-9876
E-mail: Bushwd@aol.com
Free postage in the U.K., Europe; air mail at cost.

CONTENTS

PREFACE

When Joseph Shein approached me with the idea of writing this book, he already had a concept. He had selected about 100 coverlets from his collection and wanted large color pictures of both sides of every piece – something that, to his knowledge and mine, had not previously been done. He wanted a text that would be informative but not too technical, perhaps with a focus on patriotism. The emphasis would be on the imagery. I immediately responded that these images reflect the whole spirit of pride and enthusiasm of the 19th century American. The project grew from there.

The decision to show both sides of each coverlet offered an exciting chance to illustrate the dramatic reversals of color and pattern. It presented a challenge in terms of placement of text – but we all agreed that the images should take precedence. Toward that end, the main text has been separated from "The Collection."

To provide as much room as possible for large pictures, the descriptions with each coverlet are kept short. The coverlets have been arranged in roughly chronological order, from east to west, with undated and unidentified coverlets inserted where they seem to fit best, according to these criteria. The object is to depict a tour of woven bedcovers, with emphasis on fancy coverlets, and their place in the context of American history .... History through imagery!

There were 105 coverlets selected for this book, including one overshot and one geometric double weave. The rest are fancy coverlets, woven on early barrel looms, drawlooms, or jacquard-equipped looms. There are eight states represented. Dated pieces range from 1817 to 1869. The Sheins have a particular affinity for coverlets from New York (including Long Island) and New Jersey and have acquired several early and/or rare examples.

In their collecting, the Sheins have paid special attention to the graphics of design and color as well as rarity and condition. They have faced, as we all do, the difficult and sometimes heartbreaking dilemma of "...but I may not see another one like this!" They have fared well.

—Melinda Zongor

Coverlet 33 Detail

ACKNOWLEDGMENTS

Thanks must go to Joseph and Janet Shein, for having an "eye" for what's good, for assembling a wonderful collection, for having a concept, — and for asking me to participate in this project. They have been generous with their time, receptive to ideas, and entirely delightful to work with.To Michele MacDonald, Collections Manager, The East Tennessee Historical Society, for providing information on the Maryville Woolen Mills.

To the scholars, researchers, and writers who have published indepth studies into the subject of coverlets: Dr. Clarita Anderson, Mildred Davison and Christa C. Mayer-Thurman, Susan Rabbit Goody, Eliza Calvert Hall, Catherine B. Hawthorne and Ronald L. Dotterer, John W. Heisey, Shirley Houck and Robert Bitter, Pauline Montgomery, Virginia Parslow Partridge and Rita J. Adrosko, Sandra Rambo Walker, and so many others.

To Douglas Congdon-Martin, our Senior Editor at Schiffer Publishing Ltd., who has been unfailingly patient and diplomatic with his helpful suggestions.

To Tom Morello, for his painstaking photography.

And, most of all, to the weavers themselves, who made it all possible by giving us such wonderful material to study, and whose skills, both artistic and technical, have enhanced our lives even today. Without them we would be missing something truly beautiful.

A special thank you must go to my husband, Laszlo, for his patience, research assistance and moral support through the long work hours and short deadlines, during which he had sometimes to fend for himself around the house. I couldn't have done this project without him.

To each and every one of these people, I am very grateful.

— Melinda Zongor

INTRODUCTION

Janet and I began collecting folk art in the mid-1950s. We became interested in this aspect of American culture from our association with several folk art dealers in the Philadelphia area whom I represented as an attorney. Folk art, as the term was then used, represented a chronology of the culture of the time and was an integral part of colonial life. It included sculpture, paintings, furniture, weathervanes, toleware, chalkware, textiles, and a host of other items, both utilitarian and decorative, that were found in the common household.

We began to frequent local antique shops, attend antique shows and auctions, and visit flea markets on weekends. Weathervanes, textiles, early 18th century paintings of children, quilts, painted furniture, and porcelains were our first interests. We were attracted to the bold colors and bright patterns of quilts, but in most instances quilts lacked identification. We saw our first coverlets at the 1988 Hirschl & Adler Folk Gallery exhibit in New York. The show was curated by Melinda (Ventre) Zongor, who became a good friend and mentor. We were greatly impressed with both her extensive knowledge on the subject of coverlets and her integrity, two essentials for a fine dealer. Thus, it is only proper that she write this book.

The visual, historic, and patriotic impact of the show made us instant collectors. It immediately whetted our appetites to discover more about this marvelous art form, about which we knew relatively little. We first believed that the coverlets we saw were copies; but upon questioning Melinda, she assured us they were of the period.

Here are textiles of beauty which represent an important part of the history of this country. Symbols such as the American eagle, the flag, historic buildings, weaving of presidents' faces and other patriotic images abound. Many coverlets not only contain the names of the weavers with the date, the state, and county where they were made, but also have expressions such as *United We Stand*, *Independence*, *Liberty*, *E Pluribus Unum* and numerous others. There are coverlets spanning every phase of American life. Most coverlets come in blue and white; but many are in red, green, tan, brown, and other color mixtures. All in all, they are identifiable, attractive, and desirable.

Our earliest dated coverlet is from 1817 and our latest dates to 1869. We like the fact that coverlets are two-sided, often with striking contrasts, and we enjoy using the dark sides in winter and the light sides in summer.

In our collecting, we feel that content, color, and condition are essential. Content includes historical relevance, overall design, and rarity. Color adds a visual and emotional impact. Condition must be "mint" or close to it.

We find coverlets mainly at antique shows, some at auction, and others we purchase privately through reliable dealers and experts such as Melinda.

In our opinion they are an important part of America representing our culture for nearly a century.

— Joseph D. Shein

Coverlet 37 Detail

PART I

COVERLETS IN HISTORY

We who love coverlets are drawn first by their bold color and graphic imagery. Then we look closer to see the intricacies of the patterns – the texture of the material, the skill of the weaving – and sometimes even the quirks of the design execution or spelling in the inscriptions. We have an insatiable desire to see more and learn more about these wonderful textiles, and the hunt for the unusual keeps us searching as if for treasure. Every new discovery of fact or image is like fitting another piece into a grand puzzle.

Who were these weavers? Where did they come from? Where did they live and work? Where did they get their inspiration for such wonderful depictions of flowers, trains, animals, buildings, heroes and patriotic symbols?

History can seem very dry when looked at in one dimension. But it comes alive when it is viewed from several angles. How do coverlets fit into the picture?

The motifs and design elements of lighting, furnishings, decorations, and everyday household implements have long served as teachers – offering clues and insight into the lives of the people who created and owned them. Figured and fancy coverlets, with their stunning skill and artistry, are the perfect expression of the bright optimism of the American spirit. They are inseparable from it. They provide a wonderful and perhaps unique snapshot of the life and time of 19th-century America. And what a time it was!

> ...study these inscriptions and designs, and you will see the history of American liberty told again in the old hand-woven coverlet.[1]

We offer herein a brief exploration of the "coverlet era" – the 19th century as illustrated in coverlets.

Pride & Exuberance

The flowering of figured and fancy coverlet production in America coincided with an era of many exciting developments. There was a new nation. It had survived two wars, the Revolutionary War (1755-1783) for independence, and the War of 1812 (-1815) for certain maritime rights. The American people had become proud citizens of the new United States and were evolving from defenders of freedom into full-fledged participants in the world experience.

The political scene was vibrant and exciting. There was a hard-won spirit of success, patriotism, national pride, and idealism. There was a feeling of prosperity, well-being, and security, and a sense that America had a bright future. People began to look forward and concentrate not only on establishing their lives, but also on improving them.

The Treaty of Paris (1783) ended Britain's control over foreign trade and opened new trade routes (including the China Trade), leading to new commerce, growing power, and leverage – without Britain as middleman, and without her high taxes. The country was growing in knowledge. An array of new inventions was making life a little easier and contributing to the growth of agriculture and industry. Industry, in turn, was gaining a firm foothold and enabling the new America to improve its lot and engage as an equal in international trade. Exotic goods flowed in from everywhere, and America had something to sell.

Inventions also contributed to domestic travel. As travel became more feasible, extensive and sometimes even comfortable, the economy grew, along with the spreading population.

The population grew, as well, with the immigration of people who brought their talent and ambition with them. Weavers of disparate backgrounds came to America. They brought their training, construction methods, design elements and color sense and molded them into new patterns and variations reflecting pride in their adopted country. The end product was something uniquely American.

"We hear of self-made men in England," wrote Thomas Low Nichols, "In America, there are scarcely any others." [2]

Necessity Is the Mother of Invention

> It has covered the sleep of bride and groom, it has warmed the new-made mother and babe, ...the homespun folds of the old blue and white...[3]
>
> ¤ ¤ ¤
>
> Ex-President James K. Polk, who died June 15, 1849, was wrapped in a silk winding sheet, and buried in an old-fashioned raised-lid style coffin, that was covered with black broadcloth. [4]
>
> ¤ ¤ ¤
>
> ...a coverlet is a better memorial than a gravestone, even though it be of granite. [5]

From cradle to grave, textiles are an important part of our everyday life. These days we tend to take cloth for granted, not appreciating its value. In early times, when everything was produced by hand, textiles were highly prized.

The art and science of cloth production required many types of expertise, from the growth or acquisition of raw material (flax, cotton or wool) to its cleaning and preparation, to the spinning and dyeing, and ultimately to the weaving. Each step in the process was long, hard work.

> It is said that eight spinners were necessary to supply one weaver with yarn...[6]

Allen H. Eaton offers something of an understatement:

> It was not... any lack in the quality of the hand product which stimulated the making of textile strands by machinery, but the fact that the operation was comparatively slow. [7]

By the 1790s in England, textile production was a major industry, but a protected one, and the exportation of machinery, skilled craftsmen, and valuable merino sheep were actively discouraged. Sheep in the Colonies were plentiful, but the majority of them were selected for hardiness and did not produce the fine wool available in England. The highly valued merino sheep were in short supply. There was a staunch pride in the (often) coarser American-made cloth, and George Washington created quite a stir when he wore a suit of American-manufactured woolen broadcloth for his first address to Congress.[8] However, most of the finer materials had to be imported. England flooded the American market with goods.[9] Although the best silks, cottons and worsteds could be imported (by people of means), the technology to produce them, could not.

After the War of Independence ended in 1783, things began slowly to change, both in America and abroad. By the 1790s the technological advances, which had been so fiercely protected and had helped make England so competitive, were threatening the job security of its laborers. Machines that speeded and increased production also reduced the need for manpower. Working conditions in the British textile industry were deteriorating, and weavers found themselves worrying about the security of their future.

In 1790, a determined young Englishman named Samuel Slater opened the first cotton mill in Pawtucket, Rhode Island after immigrating to America and constructing the machinery from memory. (President Madison's inaugural suit in 1809 was made of cotton manufactured in Pawtucket. The Slater Mill became known as "The Cradle of the American Cotton Industry" and was visited by Presidents Monroe and Jackson, among many other dignitaries.[10])

Advancements like the cotton picker and the carding machine (for wool) and the spinning jenny (for both wool and cotton) soon followed, brought into America by British immigrants. In 1793 American Eli Whitney invented the cotton gin. The speed and efficiency of these machines, many of them hand-operated, revolutionized the textile industry. They made it possible for Americans to produce cotton and wool yarns that were seed and dirt free and consistent in diameter.

Mills sprang up around New England, employing many women who had previously toiled at home. Cotton cloth was produced in some quantity by the 1820s.

The wool cloth industry, however, was slower to reach its full potential. Although power looms were in use in England by 1810 and in the United States by 1815, they were too hard on the delicate wool warp and could handle only the tougher cotton or linen fibers. In those times wool was used only for filler or weft. (The resulting cloth, called satinet, was very successful and popular.) For all-wool cloth, however, handlooms were still used.

Until the 1830s, much of the American-grown wool had been inferior to the English product. It was sufficient for coarse clothing and blankets, but fine wool cloth usually had to be imported. By 1830, through selective breeding and the opening of international free trade leading to the importation of more of the coveted Spanish merino sheep, America finally had home-grown, high quality wool.

Bedcovers As Textiles

> Generally our grandmothers dried their herbs... Often they would make small bags from worn out clothing. These bags were filled with the dried leaves, then sewn shut and placed among the bed clothing. [11]

Bedroom "furnishings," and the bed they were on, were the most important and valuable items in the household. A full complement of ticks, sheets, bolster pillows and covers, hangings and coverlet(s) was a major undertaking in labor and materials. The quality of those materials and the skill shown in their execution said a lot about the home they were in.

Until the 1790s, coverlets and their accompanying bed furnishings were still very much produced by hand. Both the cotton and wool yarns were often handspun, especially in the more remote areas, for many years after the mills were in operation. Home weavers produced overshot coverlets on simple, four-harness looms. Skilled professional weavers made more elaborate coverlets of double cloth in geometric patterns, using multi-harness looms. By the beginning of the 19th century, a few even made fancy coverlets. All were handwoven.

The elaborate designs of early figured or fancy cloth required elaborate mechanisms to produce them. Early drawlooms required a drawboy – usually a young man apprenticed to learn the trade – who was positioned at the back of the loom to lift the warp threads in prescribed groups, helping create the "shed" or opening through which the weaver threw his shuttle. This was slow and prone to error, and therefore expensive.

The Jacquard Invention

In 1804 Joseph-Marie Jacquard of Lyons, France, building on the inventions of others, came up with a device that was simpler, quicker, more efficient, and (most importantly) eliminated the need for the drawboy. This made the production of figured cloth more economical – a major development at the time. Understandably, in Britain and Europe this was considered a wonderful breakthrough by the consumer and the employer, but the weavers saw it as yet another in a long progression of threats to their job security. With tougher working conditions and the advent of steam power in England, skilled workers began fleeing to America to preserve their livelihood. Skilled British and European weavers needed a safe environment where they could work without constant threat of obsolescence. The Industrial Revolution had been a mixed blessing for them... but it proved to be a fortunate opportunity for the Americans.

In America, as in Europe, figured or fancy textiles were produced in small numbers using drawlooms and other means. The arrival of the jacquard attachment in America in the 1820s signaled the beginning of efficient (relatively), economical production of fancy coverlets in America.

More than any other household textiles, sheets, hand towels, etc., bedcovers stood out. They were often cherished showpieces. They were vehicles for displaying the maker's design and technical ability and were the pinnacle of the weaver's art. They were also, to some extent, status symbols. As coverlets moved from home craft to professional products, the homeowner could show off his/her standing by acquiring one of these graphic new examples of the latest technology.

Having won independence and securing safe trade over the open seas, America and its people were gaining a stronger foothold in a new world position. The textile industry in general, and the jacquard attachment in particular, played no small part in this evolution.

Spread of Technology

Jacquard-woven coverlets reached their peak years between 1840 and 1860. The handspun materials gradually gave way to mill yarns, and the power looms were eventually perfected enough to take over for the handweavers. But by then, the Civil War was on the horizon and wool was going for uniforms. Jacquard coverlet production all but ceased.

Images of the period show coverlets during the War, in the tents of the sick and wounded, perhaps supplied by local ladies anxious to support their soldiers.

After the War, coverlets took on a new look. The new looms were larger and enabled seamless construction to replace the former system of two lengths sewn together. Coal-tar-based synthetic aniline dyes, invented in the 1850s, with their acidic and sometimes garish tones, began to replace the warm colors of natural dyes. Pattern motifs changed with the times. The last postwar phase could be judged an inferior one in terms of finished mechanized product. Like many things whose time has passed, the craft of the fancy coverlet handweaver was eventually overtaken by "progress."

The Coverlet as Handicraft

It is important to note that handspun, handwoven cloth and bedcovers would be produced in at least parts of America for many years after the beginning of these great developments. Although milled cotton and wool yarns were fairly readily available by the 1830s in the eastern coastal areas, it was not the case for everyone. In the towns outside these areas, improvements were slower to arrive. As with all changes, one has to remember that things take time to filter down to the most rural and the poorest locations. This was certainly true of textile production. Long after the peak years of the fancy coverlet, humble overshot coverlets were produced well into the 19th century (and indeed into the 20th) in some areas.

In 1893, Berea College (Kentucky) and its President, Dr. William Frost, undertook a plan to revive the all-but-lost handicraft of coverlet weaving, with emphasis specifically on overshot pieces. Their first efforts were disappointing, as they could not duplicate the quality of material and dye or the skill required to equal the early coverlets. Upon being asked to fill orders for about six of these "duplicates," one weaver replied:[12]

> President Frost, in order to make so many kivers we will have to raise more sheep, shear them, pick and wash the wool, card it and spin it, then collect the bark and sich to color it. Then we will have to have the loom all set up, fix the warp and

beam it, then get a draft and thread the warp for the pattern we want, then tie up the loom, and then we will be ready for the weaving… It would take we'uns nigh one year or more afore we could have that many kivers wove. It's no child's play to weave a kiver, President. [13]

It would take several years, much practice, and a new appreciation "that the weaving of a coverlet required time, skill, and conscientious work"[14] before satisfactory results could be achieved. Eventually, there were several productive (and well-documented) weaving houses in the Southern Highlands, taking simple, handwoven coverlets into the 20th century.

Construction and Structure of Fancy Coverlets

It is a common misconception that all early looms were narrow. Most looms were narrow due to economic and space constrictions. One has to remember that coverlets were not the only things a weaver made. The narrow looms were easier, faster, and more economical to warp for the smaller projects. The large looms were more prone to error and were more cumbersome to work with. There were, however, some large looms capable of producing a full-width coverlet in one piece. *(See Coverlet 3 dated 1825, and Coverlet 6, dated 1831 as examples.)*

An accomplished weaver can comfortably and quickly handle fabric widths to at least 60". This, however, is not quite enough to create a full-width coverlet. After that, for wider cloth, production slows down without the availability of a (hand-operated) fly shuttle or another weaver to work with (one to throw, the other to catch each pass of the shuttle). Since this gets back into the economics of equipment and/or labor and space requirements, it makes sense that most early weavers would have built narrow looms, on which two lengths could be woven quickly and sewn together for a full-width coverlet.

There are two main types of structure seen in figured and fancy coverlets.

• **Double weave**, or double cloth, consists of two distinct layers of fabric. They can be pulled apart with the fingers. The pattern is formed by the raising or lowering of groups of threads in these layers, in a prescribed order. At the points where the threads pass from top to bottom, they hold the two layers together. Double weave coverlets can be of cotton and wool (one layer of cotton and the other of wool), or all wool (both layers wool).

This structure requires more material and labor and is therefore more expensive to produce than a single layer. Perhaps this is why some weavers offered their patterns in a choice of either single or double cloth.

(Double weave coverlets were made in geometric patterns on multiple harness looms, by professionals, before the fancy coverlets were available. The popularity of this type of coverlet overlapped with the early days of fancy coverlet weaving. It was not unheard of for a weaving "factory" to have a loom producing a geometric coverlet, next to a loom producing a fancy one.)

• **Tied-beiderwand** is a single-thickness cloth made of cotton warp, and cotton and wool weft. It has a linear or ribbed texture in its warp, often including pale blue or brown warp threads alternating with the natural, undyed ones.

Contrary to popular assumption, most 19th-century coverlets consist of wool and cotton (or all wool) – *not* linen. Either alone or combined with cotton or wool, linen was strong and durable and was used in a wide variety of textiles, but not generally for fine bedcovers. The term "linsey-woolsey" is often misused in this context. True linsey-woolsey was a textile consisting of flax, or linen, and wool, and was most often used for coarse clothing. Flax preparation was tedious, and, unlike cotton, the tough fiber resisted attempts at early mechanization. When milled cotton became available, handspun linen quickly fell out of favor. Perhaps adding to the confusion, there was another type of bedcover, Calamanco (also often incorrectly referred to as "linsey-woolsey"), consisting of two layers of wool, filled with wool, and quilted. The top layer was glazed. It generally predated fancy coverlets.

Important Note: Probably the most common error in identifying a coverlet's structure is the tendency to refer to double weaves as "summer and winter." Although it is logical to think of using a coverlet's darker side facing up in winter and its lighter side up in summer, that does not make it a summer and winter coverlet; and it should not be referred to as such. The terms "summer and winter" and "reversible" are not interchangeable. The term "summer and winter," properly used, refers to a structure, not a look. Summer and winter, the structure, is a *single* thickness, is entirely different from double weave, beiderwand, and overshot, is usually worked in geometric patterns, and is exceedingly rare in fancy coverlets.

Overshot is a structure not seen in figured and fancy coverlets. It is discussed here, however, because there is one overshot coverlet in the collection *(Coverlet 1)*. Overshot is a single layer, of cotton warp with a cotton and wool weft. It is characterized by small areas of wool "floats." These are wool threads which override the cotton threads and look somewhat like flattened, taught loops. Overshot coverlets were generally home products woven on simple looms and usually predate the availability of fancy and figured coverlets. However, the technically demanding pattern of soldiers seen in Coverlet 1 was very likely woven by a professional.

Origin and Migration of Weavers

Weavers of British (English, Irish, and Scottish) background and training most often worked with double cloth. Upon their arrival in America, they settled primarily in New York and New Jersey.

Weavers of Dutch, Huguenot, and German descent and training used beiderwand structure. The Dutch and the Huguenots tended to settle in New York (especially Long Island and Staten Island) and New Jersey. The Germans went mostly to Pennsylvania and Maryland.

As America grew and the Industrial Revolution grew with it, many weavers migrated west, taking their training, skills, patterns, and color sense with them. As a result, coverlets from the states of Kentucky, Ohio, Illinois, Indiana, and Michigan enjoy a mix of style and color. Even so, it is often easy to determine a weaver's origin just by looking at his product.

Most of the weavers of fancy coverlets were male (*see Coverlet 52 for an exception*). A lady's name in the corner block usually denotes the customer, rather than the weaver. There were, however, male customers as well; therefore, a man's name on a coverlet is not guaranteed to be that of the weaver (Coverlets 72 & 77).

A Note About Fringe

…around some of these old coverlets hangs a fringe of memories and traditions, little stories of life… [15]

Double woven coverlets from New York and New Jersey, are usually of cotton and wool and often have no fringe at all. Some have a fringe at the bottom only. Some New Jersey coverlets have the somewhat odd detail of fringe at top and bottom, but not on the sides – making them look almost like a rug. Midwestern double weave coverlets can be wool and cotton, or all wool, with fringe just at the bottom or on three sides.

Beiderwand coverlets from all the States generally have fringe on three sides. (A beiderwand coverlet without a fringe probably had one that has been lost, worn, removed or cut off.)

HISTORY IN COVERLETS

Patterns and Motifs

History, politics, and masonry jostle each other; there are churches and dwellings; the architecture of Boston Town and the architecture of the Orient, palm trees and pine trees, an American eagle… [16]

The customer who ordered a fancy coverlet would often supply the wool, but could choose from the patterns and colors offered by the weaver. Much like lighting, wallpaper, furniture, and furnishings (such as clocks) of the period, these patterns were signs of the times.

From the 1820s to the 1860s it is possible, by looking at coverlet motifs, to trace the development and tastes of the country as it experienced its new freedom, its pride and enthusiasm, its inventions, its growth and its expansion. One sees patriotic slogans and symbols, signs of security, architecture, prosperity, travel and trade, and flora and fauna, both commonplace and exotic.

Any individual coverlet can, and often does, include several of these different types of motifs.

In some early fancy coverlets the patterns seem almost primitive, but they quickly develop into elaborate and bold executions of the weaver's art. As time, taste, and fashions change, so do the patterns.

Floral motifs range from highly stylized and quilt-like, to classical urns filled with elaborate and exotic arrangements.

Patriotic slogans give way to images of inventions like the train and steamboat. Architecture ranges from "Boston Town" to proud centennial celebrations of grand structures like Memorial Hall. Animals seem visible almost everywhere and go from the powerful British lion to the exalted American eagle, with all manner of creatures in between.

The size of motifs themselves evolves from small repeats to one large central image in the field, surrounded by supporting arrangements in the corners. (Although the large central motifs are generally seen in later pieces, there is, of course, an exception to every rule – as seen in Coverlet 6, dated 1831.)

Colors range from blue and white or red and white to multi-colors. They go from the warm tones of natural dyes to the acidic shades and colors of synthetic aniline dyes.

These elements become a most interesting study when they are thought of as a timeline.

> ...the designs and inscriptions on some of these coverlets recall the day when every wind that blew eastward across the ocean brought with it a story... It was... the tale of a New World... where the land reached from ocean to ocean and the poorest man could have his share of it for the asking...[17]
>
> ¤ ¤ ¤
>
> ...the immigrant of those days did find the fulfillment of his heart's desire... the weaver likewise set up his loom and expressed his gratitude and his patriotism by weaving into a coverlet the emblems of his country...[18]

Slogans and Symbols

Slogans and symbols can be seen in border or field. They can be worked in very bold, large lettering, or they can be rather subtle. Sometimes one can overlook them, especially when they have been worked into an elaborate motif in the field.

Liberty, Independence

The importance of these words cannot be overstated. By the 1830s the words and their concept – treasonous only a few short years before, could now be not just whispered, but shouted. This was no small accomplishment for a young nation which had just, in historical terms, fought two wars for the right to use them. This was heady stuff! (Coverlets 11, 25, 27, 49, 50, 56, 64, & 101.)

Agriculture & Manufactures, Factory, Patent

These are all terms relating to the recent great advances in technology. One must remember that *agriculture* produces both food and fiber, including cotton, the most valuable of all the plant fibers. Just as an army moves on its stomach (with the clothes on its back), so goes the nation which is blessed with productive agriculture. *Agriculture*, along with *manufactures*, the other half of the equation, are what keeps the economy moving. (Coverlets 3, 46, & 75.) *Factory* includes operations of all kinds, large and small. A weaver who had perhaps three looms and two employees beside himself proudly considered his business to be a *factory*. (Coverlet 21.) He was also very pleased to be working for himself, or at least in an environment more secure and friendly than the one left behind in the old country. *Patent* – Weavers often built their own looms. The rights to use the jacquard attachment were sold in various ways, usually including a sort of license to use it within a certain geographical area, something like a franchise. Advertisements of the time allude to the weaver having recently secured the *patent* for this latest improvement. (Coverlets14, 15, 23, 44, & 72.)

E Pluribus Unum

Translated, "from many, one," was the first national motto. (Coverlets 6, 21, & 101.)

Under This We Prosper

This and various other words of wisdom, including *Unite We Stand, Divided We Fall* . (Coverlets 35 & 36.)

Flags and Banners

Flags and banners appear in coverlets, in varied settings in both field and border. Flags can be in standard or swallowtail shape (Coverlets 57, 71, 99, 101, & 102). Banners are usually worked into field patterns and sometimes include slogans such as *Liberty* or *E Pluribus Unum* within them (Coverlets 21, 96, & 101). In one case, the word *Liberty* is worked into the field pattern in a flowing manner resembling a sort of banner without borders (Coverlet 56). To see the difference, compare that with the field pattern in which the word *Liberty* is run in a more straightforward fashion (Coverlet 64). No matter what their form, flags and banners are always a happy addition and are an obvious celebration of patriotic fervor.

Masonry

The Freemasons or Masons, are a fraternal organization emphasizing high moral conduct, good citizenship and freedom of political and religious expression. John James Audubon, Paul Revere, General Lafayette, George Washington, and 50 of the 56 signers of the Declaration of Independence were Masons.[19] George Washington took his oath of office of the Presidency using a Masonic Lodge bible. Masonic Lodges proliferated in America, and Masons performed numerous civic services long before the new Government had any social programs in place.

Masonic symbols, often in combination with patriotic symbols, are found on a wide range of decorative arts made during the century between 1720 and 1820 and for a few years thereafter. As seen in coverlets, they include the compass and square (for morality and equality), the pillars (for wisdom, strength and beauty) and the lock (the importance of Masonic secrets). [20] (Coverlets 3 & 27)

Patriotism and History

Often incorporating the slogans described above, and perhaps the most graphic motifs seen in fancy coverlets, are the ones associated with patriotism and American history. The best of these designs include James Cunningham's *Washington on Horseback* (Coverlets 35 & 36), and both the *Agriculture & Manufactures...* (Coverlet 3) and the *American Independence Declared...* (Coverlet 27), often erroneously attributed to James Alexander. Other examples, several by unknown weavers, include a version of the Great Seal (Coverlet 6), the *Eagle and Stars* (Coverlet 19), the Presidents coverlet (Coverlet 37), *General Washington* (Coverlet 56), the *Capitol in Washington* (Coverlet 57), the ornate Capitol building (Coverlet 97), Ira Hadsell's *E Pluribus Unum* (Coverlet 102), Philip Schum's *Washington Hail* (Coverlet 102), and the *Memorial Hall* (Coverlet 103).

The symbol of the rooster was used to represent the original Democratic Party by the 1840s and appears in several coverlets in the collection. It is doubtful that every rooster had political connotations, especially the earlier ones; but it is interesting to be aware of this. (*See Animals, pg. 10, for more on roosters.*)

Travel

Independence, freedom and inventions led to trade, exploration, and discovery. Freedom of trade over the open seas led to new markets and their discoveries. (The popular architectural pattern motif known as "Christian & Heathen" is thought to pay homage to the China Trade.) Exploration of American soil led to even more. The exploration of western lands followed by a migrating population, which accelerated as travel and mobility became first possible, then economical. Paddlewheel and steam-driven river boats were a major improvement over the raft. The railroad was faster and more relaxing (hopefully) than horseback. The sailing ship had become more secure in its travels, free from the threat of attack and confiscation by foreign powers.

The steamboat, the railroad and the venerated sailing ship are all depicted in jacquard coverlets (Coverlets 32, 53, 87, 88, & 102.) (*See Architecture – Christian & Heathen/Boston Town*)

Animals

There is an astonishing array of animals depicted in jacquard coverlets. Domestic and wild beasts are displayed in field and border patterns. A partial list includes: horses (Coverlets 11, 30, 35, 36, 78, &102), dogs (Coverlets 7, 9, 67, 104, & 105), deer and stags (Coverlets 21, 60, 73, & 96), foxes (Coverlets 7, 9, & 67), cows (Coverlets 70 & 82), goats (Coverlet 3), snakes (Coverlet 56), birds (many varieties including roosters, turkeys, distelfinks, and more), lions, monkeys, giraffes, and more.... (*See Exotic Animals, pg.*)

Birds can be large or small and include doves or partridges and songbirds (Coverlets 7, 8, 24, 30, 47, 53, 54, 56, 62, 70, 72, 76, 78, 82, 92, 96, 102, 104, & 105). They are among the most popular motifs on jacquard coverlets. The most-often-seen include eagles, distelfinks, and birds of paradise.

Eagles are, of course, a matter of national pride. They appear in profusion in coverlets just as they appear on all manner of furnishings and decorations of the period from lighting and clock faces to wallpaper and china and even other textiles, including everything from printed cotton handkerchiefs to quilts. The spread eagle, usually with a crest or shield on his breast, is most often seen clenching an olive branch in one talon and arrows in the other, symbolizing peace and strength. The variations seem endless and can be primitive or refined. Eagles appear more often on the double-weave coverlets of British influence, that is, New York, New Jersey, the Western Reserve portions of Ohio and so on (Coverlets 3, 4, 5, 6, 7, 8, 9, 11, 13, 16, 17, 19, 20, 21, 23, 27, 28, 33, 35, 36, 40, 42, 49, 50, 51, 54, 56, 64, 65, 69, 78, 80, 82, 96, 101, 102, 103, 104, & 105).

Distelfink or thistlefinch, is a large crow-like image seen usually on borders of the single-weave (beiderwand) German-influenced coverlets, that is, Maryland, Pennsylvania, Ohio and points west (Coverlets 10, 18, 31, 34, 52, 60, 61, 73, & 74).

"Birds of Paradise," generally described as "exotic birds feeding their young in the nest," is a very popular motif of the period and is reminiscent of early tapestries. It is very popular today with coverlet collectors. The motif tends to be elaborate, and there are many variations. The number of young can vary, as can the relative positions of the adult birds. Sometimes the birds are feeding their young, but not in the nest. Another variation depicts exotic birds with no young. Color plays a big role in the look of this particular pattern and can make a dramatic difference from one coverlet to the next. It is used in both double weave and beiderwand coverlets, also having great effect on their appearance (Coverlets 63, 97, 98, 99, & 100). Compare these with Matthew Rattray's simplified motif which depicts different birds feeding their young, with no nest (Coverlets 80 & 81).

Roosters, turkeys, peacocks and peahens are seen in various combinations, in both field and border, sometimes very large in size (Coverlets 56, 91, & 92). One Pennsylvania weaver, Henry Oberly, used both a turkey and a rooster in his trademark (Coverlet 46), although similar turkeys and roosters appear as field pattern motifs in other coverlets that cannot be proven as his (Coverlet 93). Other examples of roosters include Coverlets 7, 8, 9, 14, 15, & 95. (*See Patriotic and Historic, pg. 9, for more on roosters.*)

Exotic Animals (in addition to the "Birds of Paradise"), such as giraffes (Coverlet 76), lions (Coverlets 12, 29, 41, 42, & 71), monkeys (Coverlets 3 & 27), etc. pose a question. What do they have to do with the experience of an American weaver? How would he even know about these animals, much less know what they look like?

During the Industrial Revolution in Britain, just prior to its counterpart in America, there was also something only slightly less important called the Natural History Revolution. There was a great interest in flora and fauna, and that interest carried over to the United States.

Englishman Thomas Bewick was already famous for his quadruped series of woodcuts (*The General History of Quadrupeds*, 1790), some of whose images were more accurate than others, and his two volumes of *The History of British Birds* (1790 & 1804). Darwin was on the *Beagle* from December, 1831, to October, 1836, working on his theory of natural selection. People had access to images of animals they might never have seen in person, and there was a wonder and excitement about the new discoveries. At least a couple of Thomas Bewick's woodcuts bear similarities to animals depicted in jacquard coverlets, and it seems at least possible that such wildly popular books as his, might have been available to mid-19th-century Americans.

And then there were the travelling shows – not quite circuses as we think of them today, but little caravans of a few wagons full of entertainment, hauling the odd and different animal from some far-away place. (They weren't producing shows on the scale of P.T. Barnum, but Barnum himself was travelling the countryside by 1835. His famous "Greatest Show on Earth," was launched in 1871.) In addition, the American people were exposed to a barrage of never-before-seen discoveries as each ship arrived in port with the products of new foreign trade. These exotics were even more strange and exciting for the rural American countryfolk.

There were new discoveries on American soil as well. From 1804 to 1806, the explorers Lewis and Clark had documented 116 new species in their travel and exploration of the Louisiana Purchase. James Audubon traveled the wilderness of the Missouri River and the bayou areas around Baton Rouge to produce his *Birds of America* in 1826 and *Quadrupeds of North America* in 1843.

Butterflies appear in at least two coverlets in the collection (Coverlets 67 & 76). One thinks of the silk moth... perhaps an homage to the important American silk industry in which Connecticut, Ohio and Pennsylvania had been most prominent. Coverlet 67 is from an area of the Western Reserve in Ohio. Coverlet 76 (unidentified) is likely to be from Pennsylvania or Ohio. Coincidence? Likely, although silk-related images do appear in other textiles, such as printed cotton handkerchiefs, of the period.

Architecture

Architectural images can be seen in borders and fields. They can represent trade ("Christian & Heathen"), justice and patriotism (courthouses and capitol buildings), religious freedom (churches), or the everyday stuff of taverns, schoolhouses, and homes (Coverlets 7, 8, 18, 24, 38, 39, 44, 45, 48, 49, 50, 63, 64, 70, 72, 76, 78, 79, 82, & 94). The homes can range from plain and "country" (log cabin, Coverlet 32)), to fancy and "city" (neo-classical, Coverlet 65) – all appropriate for their day. The motif "Christian & Heathen" combines pagodas and palm trees with domestic buildings and trees. A related motif is called "Boston Town," and includes just the domestic buildings and trees. Variations are endless. (Compare Coverlets 97, 98 & 99.) (*Also, see Travel, pg. 10.*)

Domed buildings, and particularly the Capitol, are a popular motif. This design in its many variations can include just a dome or the entire building (Coverlet 57), or even half repeats of a dome worked through the field pattern. It is interesting to note that domes appear in coverlets as early as 1825 (Coverlet 3), a year before the completion of the actual U.S. capitol building and as late as 1869 (Coverlets 102 & 103), in this collection. Some of the motifs take generous liberties with the "real thing," including some that look more like mosques, but all are clear in their intent. Since it is unlikely that the weavers, especially the early ones, had seen their capitol in Washington, and perhaps not even a drawing of it, they did a credible likeness of a classical structure. (Coverlets 3, 4, 5, 27, & 96)

Flowers, Fruits, and Trees: Peace and Plenty

> Looking at the designs of these coverlets is like walking in strange gardens...[21]

Florals illustrate many themes, usually conveying a feeling of well-being and calm reassurance, but always in great profusion. They can include prosperity and abundance (cornucopias, fruit, sheaves of wheat), trade (palm trees), or a tip of the hat to the old country (Scottish thistle, English rose, lilies of France).

A wide variety of species is seen in arrangements which follow the fashion of the times, from simple and stylized to classically elaborate, in an equally wide variety of baskets, urns, and pots. They appear in layouts of medallions or roundels, placed in straight lines or diagonal, or in grids or tiles. The number of repeats can vary, according to the size of the motif and the desired size of the coverlet.

Also represented are vines and bushes in floral, fruit, and fern. Trees appear often, and can be evergreen, deciduous, or leafless altogether (Coverlets 5, 7, 8, 9, 10, 16, 17, 18, 21, 23, 28, 29, 30, 31, 32, 33, 34, 39, 41, 42, 45, 47, 51, 54, 59, 60, 61, 65, 69, 70, 73, 74, 76, 82, 95, 97, 98, & 99).

Almost every coverlet has floral and/or vine arrangements in either the field or border – if not in both. They often serve as a quiet counterpoint to the more graphic elements of animal, architecture and invention. A few examples of cornucopias or fruit include Coverlets 19, 26, 70, 79, 89, 92, 93, & 101.

Odd Details

> When I discovered the John Mellinger coverlet I wrote to a friend in Pennsylvania, and he at once identified John Mellinger as an old acquaintance of his boyhood, known then as "Thread Jock," because of the threads that always stuck to his coat.[22]

Weaving, spelling and pattern errors, and other odd quirks can be a wonderfully enjoyable reminder that the weavers were human and that the system was not always perfect. Some odd details are not errors, but rather, the weaver's way of solving a problem. The occasional discovery that a weaver has placed a line of text, a row of birds or a corner block and its entire inscription upside down, makes one wonder what the weaver was thinking. In Pennsylvania, John Smith writes the word *Patent* and his initials upside down across the bottom of his coverlets. He then places the entire corner block with its inscription of his name, the date, and the customer's name, all upside down (Coverlets 14 & 15). The weaver of Coverlet 47 does the same. In New York, the weaver of Coverlet 26 inscribes the customer's name upside down near the top of the coverlet. Could this be purposeful? Do the weavers want the words read by the customers as they are in bed?

In the *Agriculture & Manufactures* coverlet (Coverlet 3), the *N* in the name *GENERAL LAFAYETTE* is backwards.

Sometimes there isn't enough space in the corner block for an entire word, so the last letter is made smaller. Samuel B. Musselman (Coverlet 77) has this problem with the letter *t* in the word *Coverlet*.

Abbreviations, some of them rather creative, are common. In the Rossville coverlet (Coverlet 72), the word "weaver" becomes *wer*. In this case, the coverlet was made in an early Dutch settlement, where his pronunciation of the letter "w" would likely have been as a "v."

The *Hemfield Railroad* coverlet (Coverlet 88) should have a letter "p" for proper spelling – but it wouldn't have fit into the space allowed. There is no way to determine if this is an imaginative abbreviation or a spelling error. Perhaps he just "sounded it out."

It is always interesting to study the spelling. G. Stich states that he *woove* his coverlets (Coverlet 39) in Newark, Ohio. Of course, perhaps he pronounced it that way! Both Christian Van Nortwic(k) (Coverlet 25) and Peter Harting (Hartung) (Coverlet 10) spell their own names two or even three different ways. Samuel B. Musselman spells the name of his town, Hilltown, as *Hiltown* (Coverlets 77 & 95). Archibald Davidson spells the word "independence" as *Independance* (Coverlet 11). Siefert & Co. (Coverlet 75) proudly advertises its *Superiour* coverlets in its corner block.

Mismatched color changes in the two sections of a coverlet, upside down or reversed pattern blocks, improperly split pattern drafts in the center motif of a field and/or border, and so on, have all been seen by the author. Errors can be as large as an entire motif or as subtle as a missed thread.

An odd detail can be seen at the bottom border of Coverlet 2 in the collection. At first glance, it appears to be a mistake, or at the least, a failed pattern attempt of some sort. Upon closer inspection, however, one sees that the left half of the border (on the light side) consists of partial repeats of the date (December 14, 1817). The right half of the bottom border (light side), which doesn't match the left half, is actually a series of partial repeats of the customer's name (Rebecca Hawkins). This is purposeful. It is the weaver's method of inscribing a double weave *geometric* coverlet *before the days of the jacquard attachment*. Coverlets of this type, all from Long Island, are consistently worked in this manner.... an interesting confirmation that quirks and oddities are not all errors.

Sometimes one can detect a color change resulting from a different dye lot of yarn being worked into the weaving. (A great study can be made of the subtleties of natural dyes and dye lots.) All of these details remind us of the touch of human hands.

From Household Furnishing to Recognition as Art

It is amazing that so many fine examples of a relatively perishable 19th-century household furnishing could have lasted until now. This is certainly a testament to the fact that coverlets were held dear in the hearts of their original and subsequent owners. Early people of vision, among them Eliza Calvert Hall (*A Book of Hand-Woven Coverlets*, 1912), and Allen H. Eaton and Doris Ulmann (*Handicrafts of the Southern Highlands*, 1937), with their beautiful prose and photography, were among the first to recognize coverlets as more than just utilitarian objects. Others followed, with their painstaking research and documentation of the weavers and their coverlets. In the modern age, there is a new appreciation for this wonderful product of the weaver's art, whose beauty surpasses its need for utility. Coverlets are now in collections, large and small, of private owners and museums around the country.

Summary

To today's eye, the design sense of the 19th-century coverlet may seem busy or even incoherent. The wild and sometimes colorful mix of the floral field with the architectural border, or the profusion of patriotic slogans and historical symbols, might be puzzling to the modern American. It is important to remember that the fancy coverlet was made in a day when patriotism was deeply felt and the concept of *Liberty* stirred people's souls. Pride in one's country was not considered corny, as, unfortunately, it so often is today. It was a day when the average person really felt that anything was possible. It was a day of excitement and freedom of expression. And it was a day when new weaving technology could express that excitement in the most vivid way, through the most cherished symbol of the home – the bedcover.

The weavers were human. They had their work ethic, their skills, their pride and their spirit, their families, their fears, their burdens and responsibilities – and their shortcomings. Through all that, they left us beauty. Coverlets are a glorious celebration of the time, the art, and the people.

> The next time you see an old coverlet just remember it is a remnant from the past. It is another piece of our American Heritage.[23]

PART II

THE COLLECTION

Joseph and Janet Shein have recognized the importance of coverlets as art. They realize that these figured and fancy American-made coverlets can usually be traced to state of origin, are uniquely identifiable and are often signed .... And, of course, they are reversible – often with dramatic results.

The Sheins have assembled over 100 coverlets into a comprehensive and varied collection, including a number of early and rare pieces, representing all the major coverlet producing states. This book will focus on 105 selections. Each is shown in full, in color, and on both sides. All but two are figured and fancy coverlets. There is one overshot and one multi-harness geometric double weave. Most are dated and range from 1817 to 1869. The identified pieces represent weavers from eight states.

The collection is arranged in chronological order, going from the eastern states to the western. Unidentified coverlets are inserted where they work best for continuity, according to their most likely date or origin.

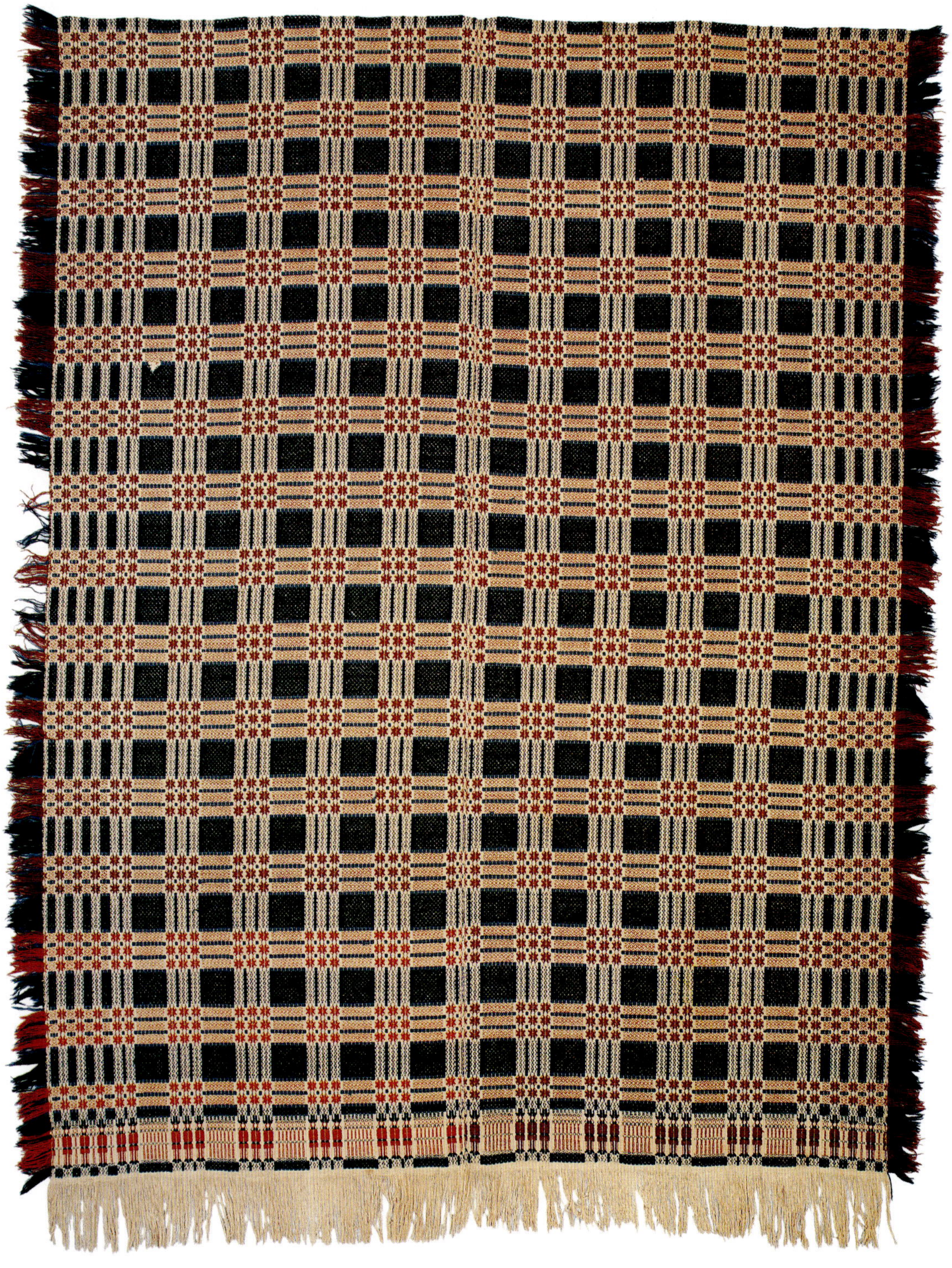

Coverlet 1
Coverlets of overshot structure were often a home product, woven by the lady of the house for her own use. However, the more complicated, multi-harness designs like this one were generally woven by professionals – usually men. Note the soldier figures in red near the bottom (foot) end. This coverlet likely predates the availability of the figured and fancy coverlets.

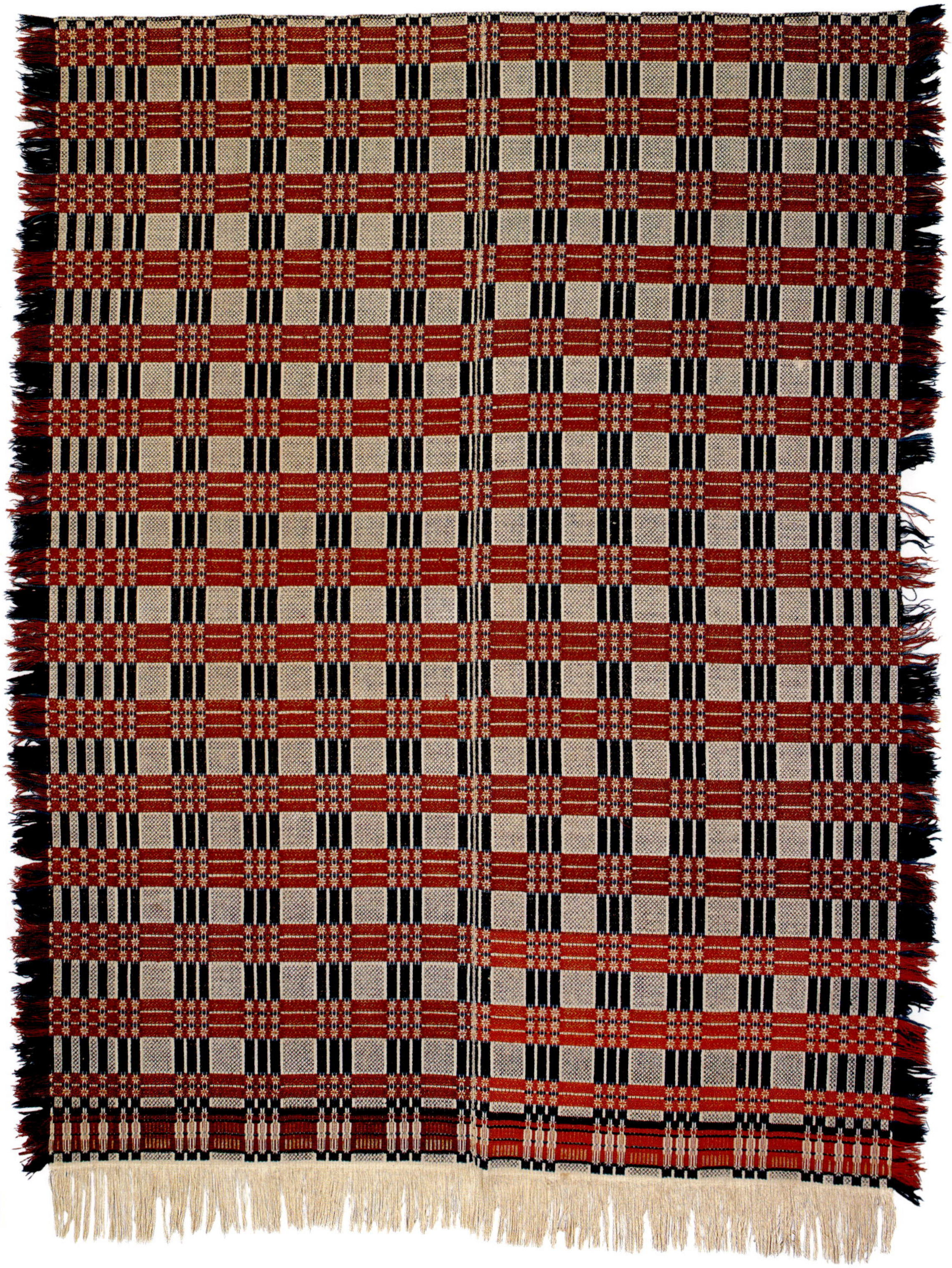

Coverlet 1 (reverse)
Weaver: unidentified.
Origin: unidentified.
Structure: overshot
Warp: natural cotton. Weft: natural cotton, red and light and dark blue wool.
Two panels joined; 101" long x 78" wide.

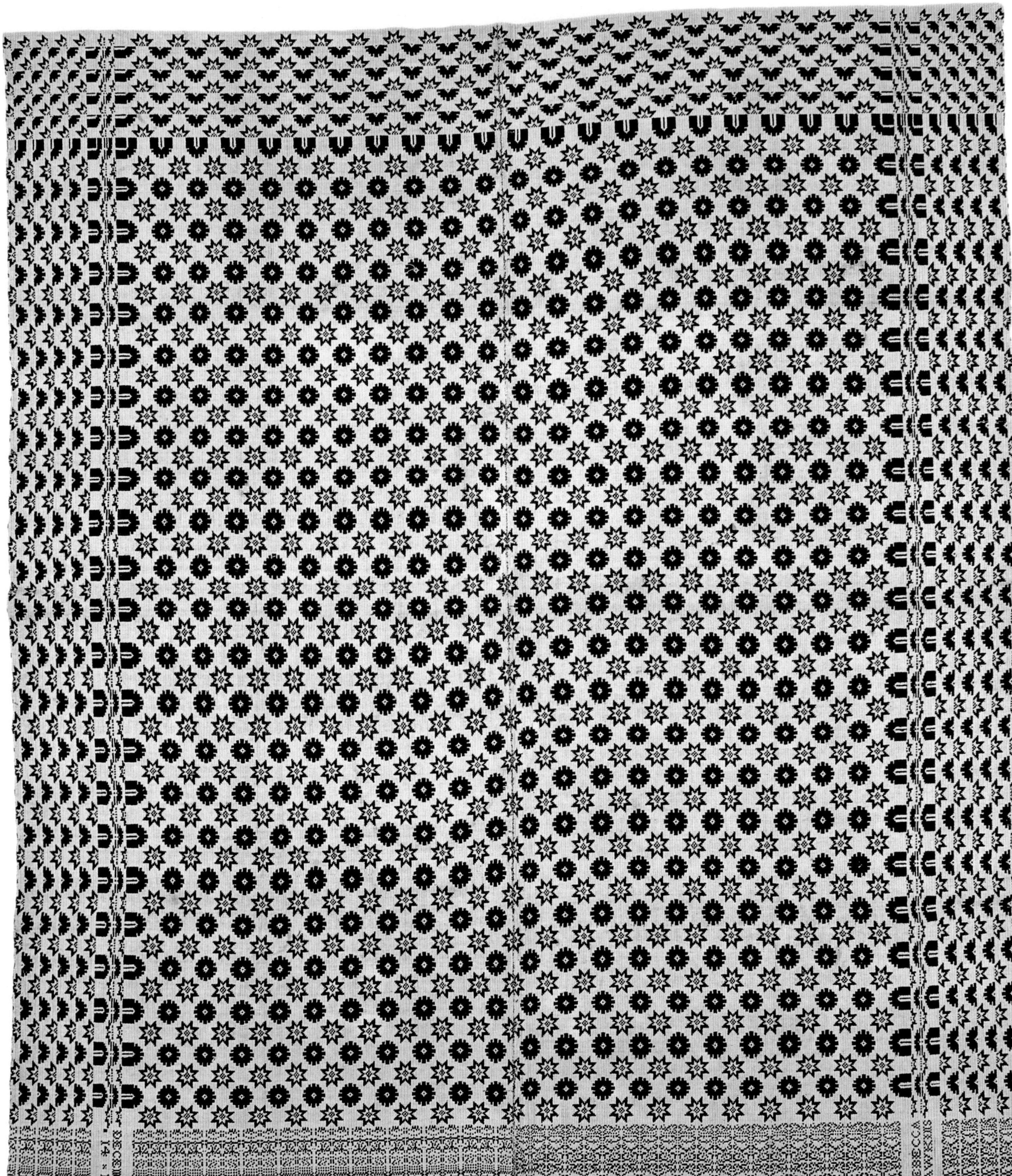

Coverlet 2
An early coverlet in geometric patterns with a name and date, is rare. Nearly all extant coverlets done in this way, with name and date in the border, have been traced to Westbury, Long Island, New York.[1] Note the strange jumble at the bottom border. It consists of partial repeats of the date on one side and the client's name on the other. Therefore the two halves of the borders do not match. This inscription can only be read correctly on the light side.

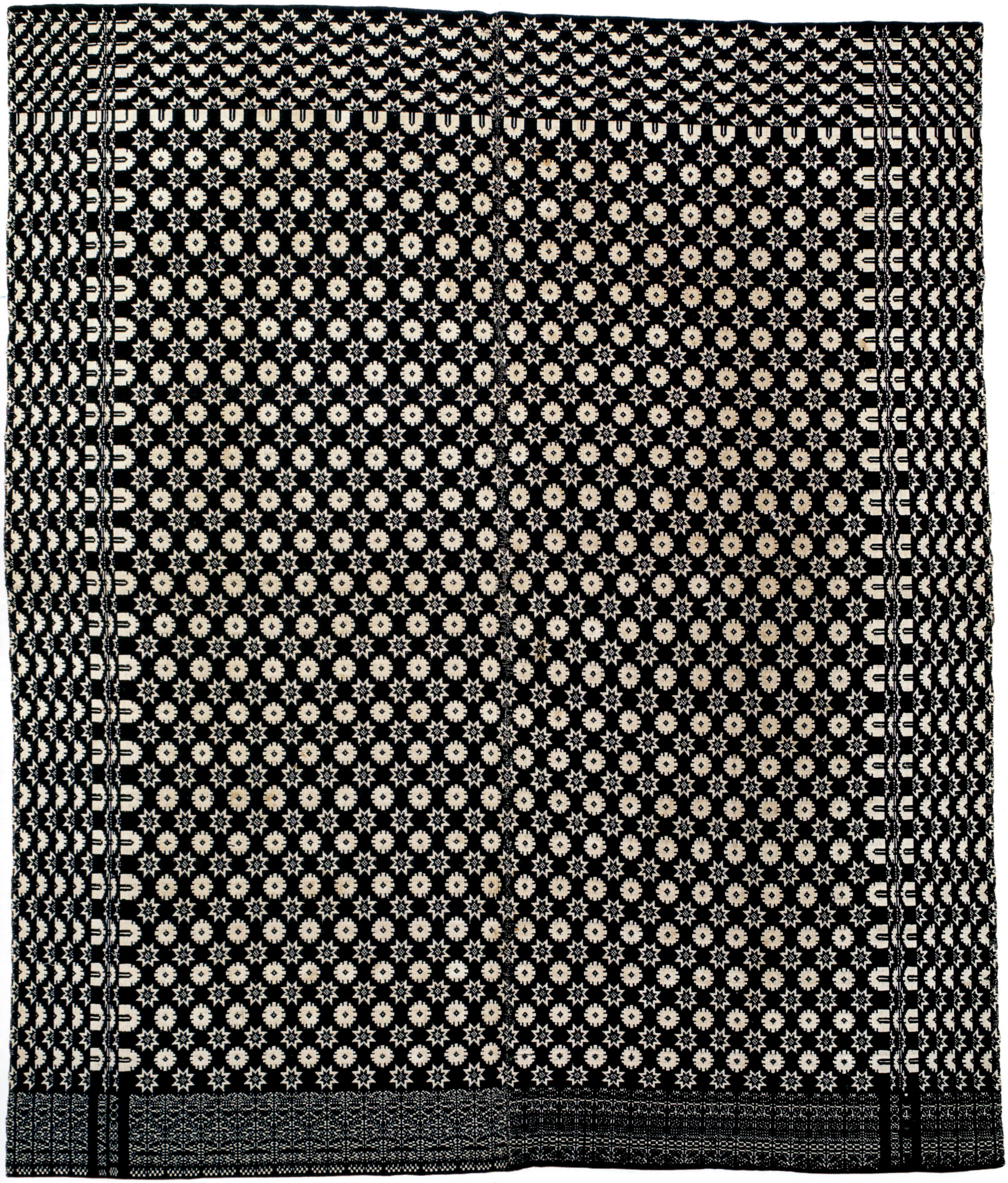

Coverlet 2 (reverse)
Weaver: unidentified.
Origin: Westbury, L.I., New York.
Client: Rebecca Hawkins
Inscrip: DECEMBER/14.1817 – REBECCA/HAWKINS
Structure: double weave
Warp: natural cotton and blue wool. Weft: natural cotton and blue wool.
Two panels joined; 93" long x 79" wide.

Coverlet 3
Coverlets like these have long been attributed to James Alexander. However, more recent research has led to the conclusion that several weavers produced this motif, with variations in the field patterns, and that Alexander did not make them. Weaver is unknown.[2]

Coverlet 3 (reverse)
Weaver: unidentified.
Origin: New York.
Client: Rhoby Boyd
Inscrip: AGRICUL/TURE & MAN/UFACTURES./ARE.THE.FOUND/ATION.OF/OUR.INDE/PENDENCE./JULY.4./1825/GnRL LAFAYETTE/RHOBY BOYD
Structure: double weave
Warp: natural cotton and blue wool. Weft: natural cotton and blue wool.
One panel; 96" long x 72" wide.

Coverlet 4
It is not known whether B. Fletcher is the weaver or the client, but probably the client. This coverlet and the next (Coverlet 5) share many details and were possibly made by the same weaver. Note the interesting partial repeats of the capitol domes as they are carried into the field pattern.

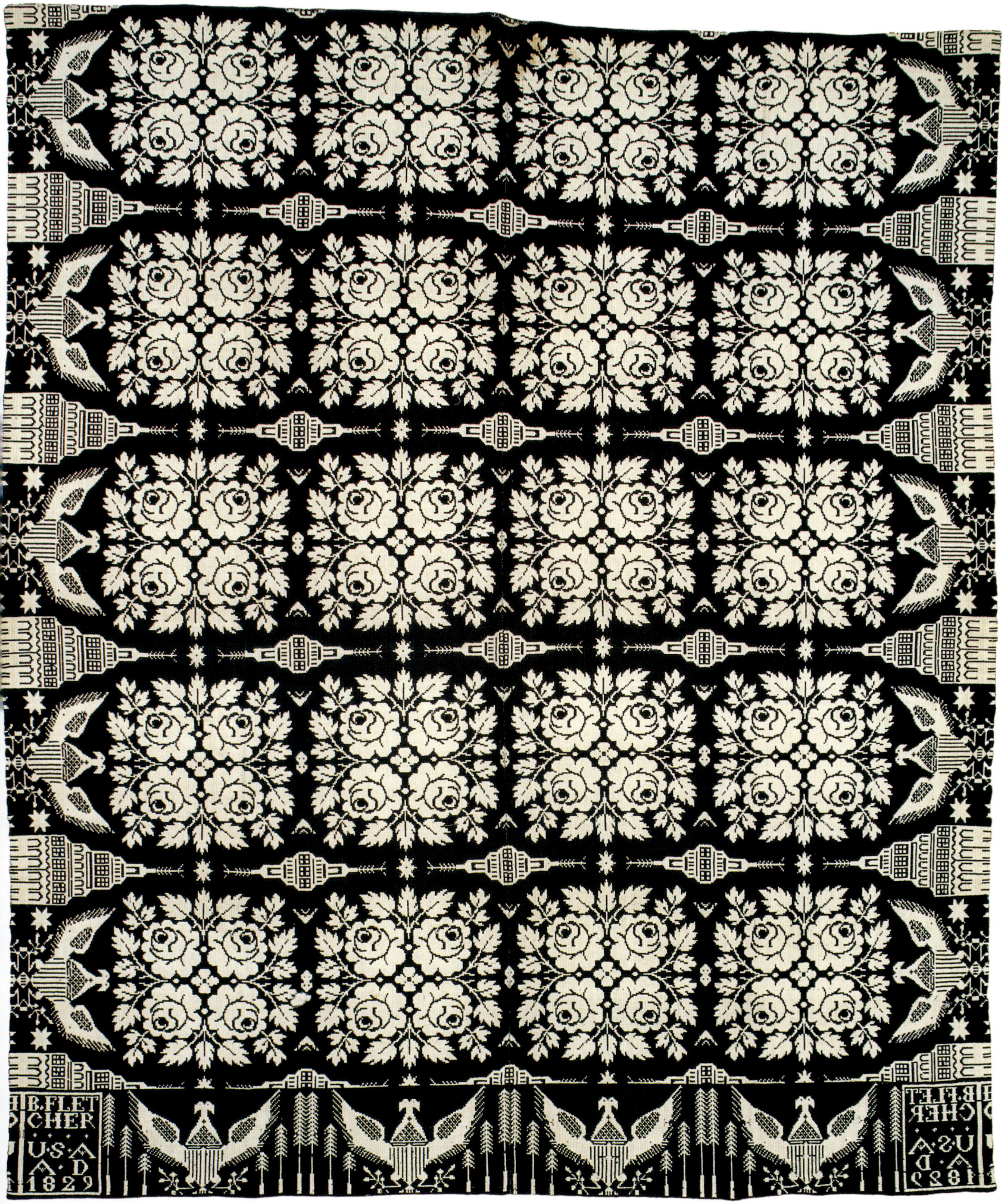

Coverlet 4 (reverse)
Weaver: unidentified.
Origin: New York.
Client: B. Fletcher (?)
Inscrip: B.FLET/CHER/U.S.A/A.D/1829
Structure: double weave
Warp: natural cotton and blue wool. Weft: natural cotton and blue wool.
Two panels joined; 89" long x 77" wide.

Coverlet 5
H. Lamb is probably the client.

Coverlet 5 (reverse)
Weaver: unidentified.
Origin: Benton, Orange Co., New York.
Client: H. Lamb (?)
Inscrip: H/LAMB/BENTON/NY.1830
Structure: double weave
Warp: natural cotton and blue wool. Weft: natural cotton and blue wool.
Two panels joined; 88" long x 79" wide.

Coverlet 6
A coverlet this early in one panel (seamless) and with a large central motif is unusual. These characteristics are more often associated with much later examples, c. 1860. The stylized stars in the field are reminiscent of geometric-patterned coverlets, while the rest of the design is more classical – an interesting mix. Some liberties have been taken with the accuracy of this version of the United States Seal.

Coverlet 6 (reverse)
Weaver: unidentified.
Origin: New York (attr.).
Inscrip: UNITED STATES OF AMERICA/E PLURIBUS UNUM/1831
Structure: double weave
Warp: natural cotton and blue wool. Weft: natural cotton and blue wool.
One panel, seamless; 93" long x 72" wide.

Coverlet 7
Though not signed by the weaver, these are generally attributed to David Haring. Compare the pattern motifs and inscriptions on this, with the next two coverlets (Coverlets 8 & 9).

Coverlet 7 (reverse)
Weaver: David Haring (attrib).
Origin: Norwood, Bergen Co., New Jersey.
Inscrip: RAT/Feb11/1831.
Structure: double weave
Warp: natural cotton and blue wool. Weft: natural cotton and blue wool.
Two panels joined; 92" long x 71" wide.

Coverlet 8

Coverlet 8 (reverse)
Weaver: David Haring (attrib).
Origin: Norwood, Bergen Co., New Jersey.
Inscrip: EA/April 2/1832
Structure: double weave
Warp: natural cotton and blue wool. Weft: natural cotton and blue wool.
Two panels joined; 99" long x 70" wide.

Coverlet 9

These pattern motifs and the small rose in the corner block are used by I. Christie (sometimes spelled Christy) as well as David Haring, both of Bergen County, New Jersey. Sometimes these coverlets are also signed; and unless they are, it is difficult to be sure which man made the piece. However, they are generally attributed to David Haring.

Coverlet 9 (reverse)
Weaver: David Haring.
Origin: Norwood, Bergen Co., New Jersey.
Inscrip: JANE.HOPPER/ZABRISKIE/1833
Structure: double weave
Warp: natural cotton and blue wool. Weft: natural cotton and blue wool.
Two panels joined; 98" long x 73" wide.

Coverlet 10
Peter Harting spells his name variously as Harting and Hartung. In this case, he adds an extra "T."

Coverlet 10 (reverse)
Weaver: Peter Harting (Hartung).
Origin: Vera Cruz, Lancaster Co., Pennsylvania.
Inscrip: PETER/HART/TUNG/1834
Structure: tied-beiderwand
Warp: natural cotton. Weft: natural cotton and red and blue wool.
Two panels joined; 101" long x 84" wide.

Coverlet 11
Archibald Davidson's prominent use of the thistle indicates his Scottish heritage, as does the double weave structure. Note his spelling of the word "independence." Compare the patterns and corner block of this, with Coverlet 21.

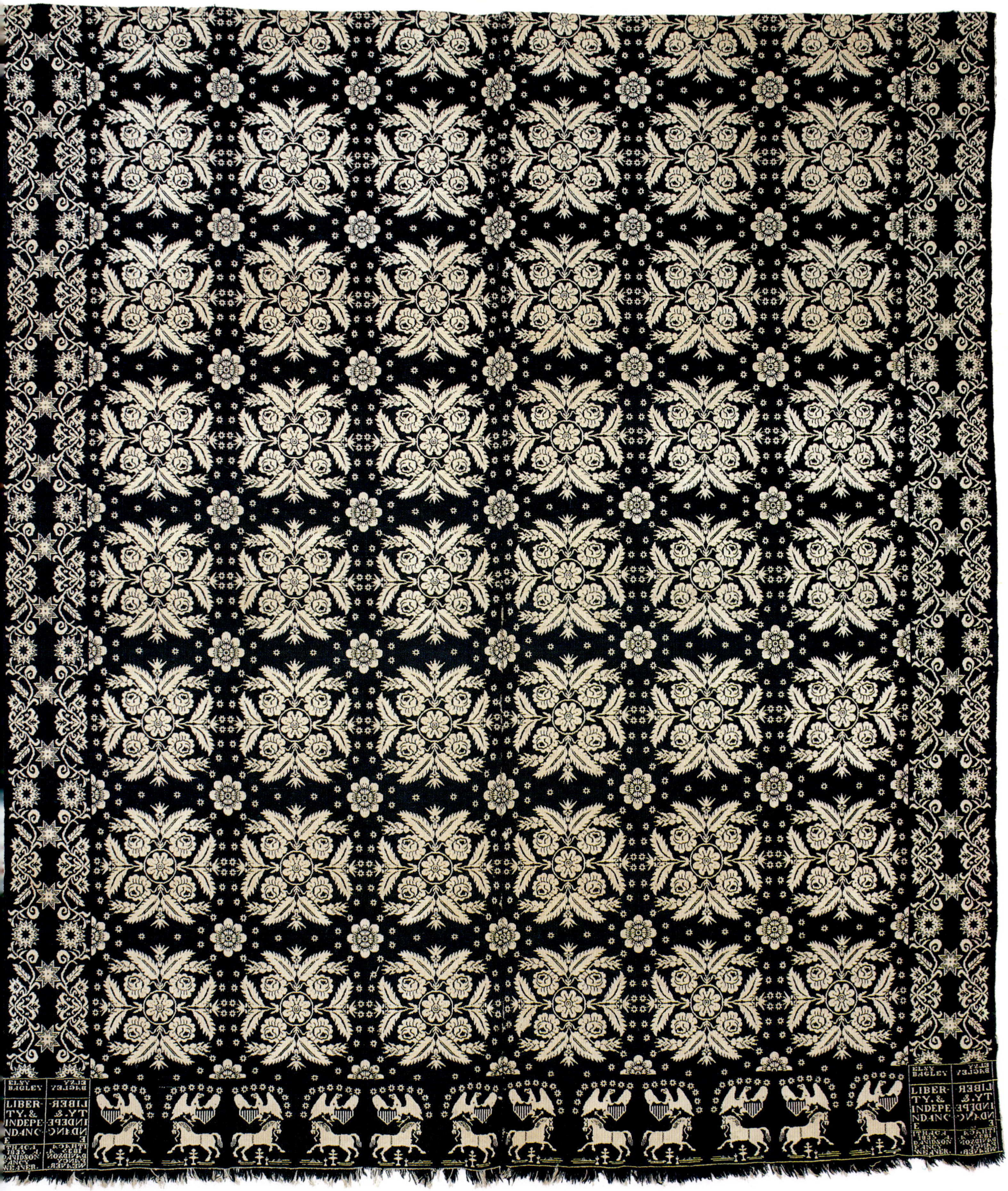

Coverlet 11 (reverse)
Weaver: Archibald Davidson.
Origin: Ithaca, Tompkins Co., New York.
Client: Elsy Bagley
Inscrip: ELSY/BAGLEY/LIBER-/TY.&/INDEPE/NDANC-/E/ITHACA/1835 A./DAVIDSON/FANCY/WEAVER.
Structure: double weave
Warp: natural cotton and blue wool. Weft: natural cotton and blue wool.
Two panels joined; 88" long x 79" wide.

Coverlet 12
Bartlett French and Harry Tyler are the two weavers who use lions, but they use them differently. French has them in his borders. Tyler has them for his trademark. (Compare this coverlet with Tyler's – Coverlets 29, 41, & 42.)

Coverlet 12 (reverse)
Weaver: Bartlett French.
Origin: Waterville, Oneida Co., New York.
Client: Esther Cutler
Inscrip: ESTHER/CUTLER.1835/B./FRENCH/WEAVER/WATER/-VILLE.
Structure: double weave
Warp: natural cotton and blue wool. Weft: natural cotton and blue wool.
Two panels joined; 91" long x 77" wide.

Coverlet 13
This coverlet is virtually a duplicate of Coverlet 20, except for the different dates and the very small, different, initials which appear in one corner of both pieces. They also differ in the number of pattern repeats in the field. They are probably by the same weaver.

Coverlet 13 (reverse)
Weaver: unidentified.
Origin: New York.
Inscrip: 1836 (initialed AM or AH in one corner)
Structure: double weave
Warp: natural cotton and blue wool. Weft: natural cotton and blue wool.
Two panels joined; 91" long x 84" wide.

Coverlet 14
This coverlet and the next one (Coverlet 15) were made for sisters. Note that the inscriptions and corner blocks on both coverlets are upside down. Compare the colors.

Coverlet 14 (reverse)
Weaver: John Smith.
Origin: Schaefferstown, Heidelberg Twp., Lebanon Co., Pennsylvania.
Client: H. Walder
Inscrip: JOHN/SMITH/1836/H./WALDER/J.S.PATENT
Structure: tied-beiderwand
Warp: natural and blue cotton. Weft: natural cotton and red, blue, and green wool.
Two panels joined; 102" long x 90" wide.

Coverlet 15

Coverlet 15 (reverse)
Weaver: John Smith.
Origin: Schaefferstown, Heidelberg Twp., Lebanon Co., Pennsylvania
Client: L. Walder
Structure: tied-beiderwand
Warp: natural and blue cotton. Weft: natural cotton and red, blue, and teal wool.
Two panels joined; 103" long x 89" wide.

Coverlet 16
Compare this coverlet with the next one (Coverlet 17) by the same weaver. Other than identical borders, the use of color and pattern is quite different.

Coverlet 16 (reverse)
Weaver: Jacob Shalk
Origin: Lebanon, Lebanon Co., Pennsylvania.
Client: M.B.
Inscrip: JACOB/SHALK/M.B/1836
Structure: tied-beiderwand
Warp: natural and blue cotton. Weft: natural cotton and red, blue, and pale green wool.
Two panels joined; 97" long x 80" wide.

Coverlet 17

Coverlet 17 (reverse)
Weaver: Jacob Shalk.
Origin: Lebanon, Lebanon Co., Pennsylvania.
Inscrip: JACOB/SHALK/1837
Structure: tied-beiderwand
Warp: natural and blue cotton. Weft: natural cotton and red, blue, and green wool.
Two panels joined; 96" long x 88" wide.

Coverlet 18

Coverlet 18 (reverse)
Weaver: John Royer.
Origin: New Holland, Lancaster Co., Pennsylvania.
Inscrip: JOHN/ROYER/NEW HOLLAND/1837
Structure: tied-beiderwand
Warp: natural and blue cotton. Weft: natural cotton and red, blue, and green wool.
Two panels joined; 91" long x 86" wide.

Coverlet 19
A patriotic theme of eagles and stars surrounds images of cavalrymen with swords drawn. Their classic pose, the floral background, and the eagles convey a message of success. Compare these soldiers with the ones in Coverlet 1 and the well-known Washington on Horseback (Coverlets 35 & 36).

Coverlet 19 (reverse)
Weaver: unidentified.
Origin: New York.
Inscrip: EAGLE & STARS/1838
Structure: double weave
Warp: natural cotton and blue wool. Weft: natural cotton and blue wool.
Two panels joined; 86" long x 72" wide.

Coverlet 20

Coverlet 20 (reverse)
Weaver: unidentified.
Origin: New York.
Inscrip: 1838 (initialed AP in one corner)
Structure: double weave
Warp: natural cotton and blue wool. Weft: natural cotton and blue wool.
Two panels joined; 93" long x 79" wide.

Coverlet 21
The term "factory" might refer to as few as two or three looms under one roof – it does not have the same connotation it would today. Many weavers produced ingrain carpeting.

Coverlet 21 (reverse)
Weaver: Archibald Davidson.
Origin: Ithaca, Tompkins Co., New York.
Inscrip:WOVEN/AT/THE/ITHACA/CARPET/FACTORY/BY/ARCH.D/DAVIDSON/1838.
Structure: double weave
Warp: natural cotton and blue wool. Weft: natural cotton and blue wool.
Two panels joined; 96" long x 79" wide.

Coverlet 22
This John Smith coverlet is very different from those illustrated earlier (Coverlets 14 & 15).

Coverlet 22 (reverse)
Weaver: John Smith.
Origin: Schaefferstown, Heidelberg Twp., Lebanon Co., Pennsylvania.
Client: J. Gackly
Inscrip: JOHN.SMITH/J.GACKLY/1838
Structure: tied-beiderwand
Warp: natural and blue cotton. Weft: natural cotton and red, blue, and green wool.
Two panels joined; 92" long x 84" wide.

Coverlet 23
Note the double corner blocks and the inverted eagles.

Coverlet 23 (reverse)
Weaver: Martin Hoke.
Origin: Dover, York Co., Pennsylvania.
Client: L. Weigel
Inscrip: M.HOKE/IN/DOVER/1838/L.WEIGEL/PATENT
Structure: tied-beiderwand
Warp: natural and blue cotton. Weft: natural cotton and red, blue, and green wool.
Two panels joined; 103" long x 82" wide.

Coverlet 24
A portion of the corner block has been left open to accommodate the name of a client.

Coverlet 24 (reverse)
Weaver: I. Myer (full name unknown).
Origin: Millersville, Lancaster Co., Pennsylvania.
Inscrip: PROPERTY./OF.(blank)/1838/WOVE.BY./I.MYER.
Structure: tied-beiderwand
Warp: natural cotton. Weft: natural cotton and red, blue, and green wool.
Two panels joined; 86" long x 81" wide.

Coverlet 25
Christian Van Nortwic(k) owner and operator of the Ark Factory on the Musconetcong River in Asbury until 1850, spells his name variously, with and without the "k." When the "k" does appear, it is usually much smaller and appears squeezed into the corner block.

Coverlet 25 (reverse)
Weaver: Christian Van Nortwic(k).
Origin: Asbury, Warren Co., New Jersey.
Client: Hannah Maria Winter
Inscrip:HANNAH/MARIA/WINTER/ASBURY/1839.C.VAN/NORTWIC/FANCY/WEAVER./LIBERTY
Structure: double weave
Warp: natural cotton and red wool. Weft: natural cotton and red wool.
Two panels joined; 86" long x 81" wide.

Coverlet 26
About three different pattern styles, including this one, have been attributed to Nathaniel Young. Little is known about him, and his coverlets are seldom signed. This attribution is based on a similar coverlet containing the initials NY. Notice that the inscription of the client's name is upside down, near the top (head) end – perhaps intended to be read by her while she was in bed!

Coverlet 26 (reverse)
Weaver: Nathaniel Young (attrib).
Origin: (probably) Bergen Co., New Jersey.
Client: Rebekah Maysinger
Inscrip: REBEKAH/MAYSINGER
Structure: double weave
Warp: natural cotton and blue wool. Weft: natural cotton and blue wool.
One panel, seamless; 98" long x 73" wide.

Coverlet 27
As with Coverlet 3, these coverlets are often erroneously attributed to James Alexander. Weaver is unknown.

Coverlet 27
Weaver: unidentified.
Origin: New York.
Client: EFH
Inscrip:AMERIC/AN.INDE/PENDEN/CE.DECL/ARED.JU/LY.4.1776/WOVE/IN/1839/EFH
Structure: double weave
Warp: natural cotton and blue wool. Weft: natural cotton and blue wool.
Two panels joined; 87" long x 78" wide.

Coverlet 28

Coverlet 28 (reverse)
Weaver: Jacob Impson.
Origin: Cortland Co., New York.
Inscrip: IMPSON/1839/CORTLAND COUNTY
Structure: double weave
Warp: natural cotton and blue wool. Weft: natural cotton and blue wool.
Two panels joined; 92" long x 85" wide.

Coverlet 29

Harry Tyler's trademark lions vary in style, size, and orientation in his corner blocks (compare with Coverlets 41 & 42). In later coverlets, his lions are replaced with various eagles (see Coverlet 51). Tyler is known for the unique variety of his patterns and the quality of his colors. His work is a perfect study of pattern, which changed and evolved with the fashion of the day. His early work is highly stylized and quilt-like, developing later into classical floral and foliate designs. The author has seen Tyler coverlets of red, burgundy, salmon, blue, mustard yellow, and dark green wool (all, of course, with natural cotton). It is unusual to see two client names on a coverlet. This one was made for Patience and Emily Ely, possibly to celebrate their birth.

Coverlet 29 (reverse)
Weaver: Harry Tyler.
Origin: Butterville, Jefferson Co., New York.
Clients: Patience and Emily Ely
Inscrip: PATIENCE ELY/EMILY ELY/1839/JEFFERSON.CO.NY.
Structure: double weave
Warp: natural cotton and red wool. Weft: natural cotton and red wool.
Two panels joined; 89" long x 81" wide.

Coverlet 30

Coverlet 30 (reverse)
Weaver: unidentified.
Origin: Reading, Schuyler Co., New York.
Client: Rebecca Trimmer
Inscrip: REBECCA/TRIMMER/READING/1839
Structure: double weave
Warp: natural cotton and blue wool. Weft: natural cotton and blue wool.
Two panels joined; 87" long x 75" wide.

Coverlet 31

Coverlet 31 (reverse)
Weaver: unidentified.
Origin: unidentified.
Inscrip: 1839
Structure: tied-beiderwand
Warp: natural and blue cotton. Weft: natural cotton and red and blue wool.
Two panels joined; 89" long x 73" wide.

Coverlet 32
Three of the four Gilmour brothers, Gabriel, Joseph, and William, were weavers. (Thomas preferred farming and left the family business.) The wonderful sailing ship trademark is uniquely theirs, as is the charming and sturdy-looking country house.

Coverlet 32 (reverse)
Weaver: Gilmour Family.
Origin: Dunlapsville, Union Co., Indiana.
Inscrip: YEAR 1839
Structure: double weave
Warp: natural cotton and blue wool. Weft: natural cotton and blue wool.
Two panels joined; 91" long x 73" wide.

Coverlet 33
Compare this with Coverlet 54, made six years later.

Coverlet 33 (reverse)
Weaver: Asahel Amora Phelps.
Origin: Delhi, Delaware Co., New York.
Inscrip: DELHI/1840
Structure: double weave
Warp: natural cotton and blue wool. Weft: natural cotton and blue weft.
Two panels joined; 94" long x 78" wide.

Coverlet 34

Coverlet 34 (reverse)
Weaver: John Denholm.
Origin: Pennsylvania (exact location unknown).
Inscrip: MADE.BY/J.DENHOLM/1840
Structure: tied-beiderwand
Warp: natural cotton. Weft: natural cotton and red, blue, and celery green wool.
Two panels joined; 94" long x 84" wide.

Coverlet 35
James Cunningham's Washington on Horseback is one of the best examples of historic and patriotic motifs used in fancy coverlets. Note the client's name at the top (head) end, and the maker's name and location at the bottom (foot) end.

Coverlet 35 (reverse)
Weaver: James Cunningham.
Origin: New Hartford, Oneida Co., New York.
Client: Esther Cutler
Inscrip: ESTHER CUTLER/1841/UNITED/WE/STAND/DIVIDED/WE/FALL/WASHINGTON/ J.CUNNINGHAM/WEAVER.N.HARTFORD/ONEIDA.Co.N.YORK/UNDER THIS WE PROSPER
Structure: double weave
Warp: natural cotton and blue wool. Weft: natural cotton and blue wool.
Two panels joined; 84" long x 74" wide.

Coverlet 36
This version of the Washington on Horseback has no client name at the top (head) end. Instead, there is an additional half repeat of the field pattern motif, and the coverlet is several inches longer than Coverlet 35, perhaps to allow for a pillow bolster.

Coverlet 36 (reverse)
Weaver: James Cunningham.
Origin: New Hartford, Oneida Co., New York.
Inscrip:1841/UNITED/WE/STAND/DIVIDED/WE/FALL/WASHINGTON/J.CUNNINGHAM/WEAVER.N.HARTFORD/ONEIDA.C<u>o</u>.N.YORK/UNDER THIS WE PROSPER
Structure: double weave
Warp: natural cotton and red wool. Weft: natural cotton and red wool.
Two panels joined; 91" long x 73" wide.

Coverlet 37
The borders around this coverlet include profile images of the Presidents Washington, Madison, Monroe, Adams, Van Buren, Jackson and Harrison. The weaver and origin are unknown.

Coverlet 37 (reverse)
Weaver: unidentified.
Origin: unidentified.
Inscrip: WASHINGTON/MADISON/MONROE/ ADAMS/VAN BUREN/JACKSON/HARRISON
Structure: tied-beiderwand
Warp: natural and brown cotton. Weft: natural cotton and red and olive green wool.
One panel, seamless; 90" long x 91" wide.

Coverlet 38

Coverlet 38
Weaver: Benjamin Lichty.
Origin: Bristol, Wayne Co., Ohio.
Inscrip: WOVE BY/BANJAMIN/LICHTY./BRISTOL/CO./.OHIO./1841
Structure: tied-beiderwand
Warp: natural and blue cotton. Weft: natural cotton and blue wool.
Two panels joined; 93" long x 78" wide.

Coverlet 39
This coverlet is standard G. Stich work, with his characteristic spelling, his bright colors, and his very large and bold pattern repeats in both field and border.

Coverlet 39 (reverse)
Weaver: G. Stich (full name unknown).
Origin: Newark, Licking Co., Ohio.
Inscrip: WOOVE/AT./NEWARK/OHIO/1841
Structure: double weave
Warp: natural cotton and red and blue wool. Weft: natural cotton and red and blue wool.
Two panels joined; 87" long x 79" wide.

Coverlet 40

Coverlet 40 (reverse)
Weaver: Cockefair Mills.
Origin: Harmony Township, Union Co., Indiana.
Inscrip: 1842
Structure: double weave
Warp: natural cotton and blue wool. Weft: natural cotton and blue wool.
Two panels joined; 94" long x 73" wide.

JEFFERSON.CO.NY.
JEFFERSON.CO.CO.
JEFFERSON.CO.CO.
JEFFERSON.CO.NY.
DIANA FULLER 1843
DIANA FULLER 1843

Coverlet 41

Coverlet 41 (reverse)
Weaver: Harry Tyler.
Origin: Butterville, Jefferson Co., New York.
Client: Diana Fuller
Inscrip: DIANA/FULLER/1843
Structure: double weave
Warp: natural cotton and blue wool. Weft: natural cotton and blue wool.
Two panels joined; 88" long x 79" wide.

Coverlet 42
There appears to be an attempt at an inscription along the bottom of this coverlet, but it does not form letters. Since Tyler was a skilled weaver, this cannot easily be explained. Compare the field and border patterns with Coverlet 41.

Coverlet 42 (reverse)
Weaver: Harry Tyler.
Origin: Butterville, Jefferson Co., New York.
Client: R.T.
Inscrip: 1843
Structure: double weave
Warp: natural cotton and blue wool. Weft: natural cotton and blue weft.
Two panels joined; 84" long x 90" wide.

Coverlet 43

Coverlet 43 (reverse)
Weaver: Casper Peterman.
Origin: Brandywine, Chester Co., Pennsylvania
Client: Sarah Parker
Inscrip: SARAH.PARKER.1843.C.PETERMAN. BRANDYWINE.C.C.PA.
Structure: tied-beiderwand
Warp: natural cotton. Weft: natural cotton and red, blue and brown wool.
Two panels joined; 89" long x 83" wide.

Coverlet 44

Coverlet 44 (reverse)
Weaver: Martin Hoke.
Origin: Dover, York Co., Pennsylvania
Client: C. Keller
Inscrip: M.HOKE/YORK.PA/1843./C./KELLER./STYLE.PATENT.
Structure: tied-beiderwand
Warp: natural and blue cotton. Weft: natural cotton and red, blue and green wool.
Two panels joined; 106" long x 93" wide.

Coverlet 45

Coverlet 45 (reverse)
Weaver: Daniel Bury.
Origin: New Portage, Summit Co., Ohio
Inscrip: DANIEL/BURY./NEW/PORTAGE/OHIO.1843
Structure: tied-beiderwand
Warp: natural and blue cotton. Weft: natural cotton and red, blue, and mustard wool.
One panel, seamless; 84" long x 81" wide.

Coverlet 46
Henry Oberly uses a perching turkey and a small rooster in his trademark corner blocks. These birds are used by other weavers as well; and coverlets which have them in the field pattern (Coverlet 93) cannot necessarily be attributed to Oberly.

Coverlet 46 (reverse)
Weaver: Henry Oberly.
Origin: Womelsdorf, Berks Co., Pennsylvania
Client: C. Rick
Inscrip: MANUFACTURED.BY/HENRY.OBERLY/WOMELSDORF.PENN/C.RICK
Structure: tied-beiderwand
Warp: natural and blue cotton. Weft: natural cotton and red, blue, and green wool.
Two panels joined; 91" long x 77" wide.

Coverlet 47
R. Griner is likely to be the client, as other coverlets appear with the same corner block arrangement, and with other names inscribed upside-down like this one.

Coverlet 47 (reverse)
Weaver: Unidentified.
Origin: Pennsylvania (attrib.).
Client: R. Griner
Inscrip: R.GRINER.1844
Structure: tied-beiderwand
Warp: natural and blue cotton. Weft: natural cotton and red, blue, and green wool.
Two panels joined; 88" long x 85" wide.

Coverlet 48

Coverlet 48 (reverse)
Weaver: Unidentified.
Origin: Unidentified.
Structure: tied-beiderwand
Warp: natural and blue cotton. Weft: natural cotton and red and blue wool.
Two panels joined; 82" long x 80" wide.

Coverlet 49
This coverlet and the next one (Coverlet 50) are clearly by the same unknown weaver, as denoted by the identical trademark corner blocks.

Coverlet 49 (reverse)
Weaver: Unidentified.
Origin: Unidentified.
Inscrip: LIBERTY
Structure: tied-beiderwand
Warp: natural cotton. Weft: natural cotton and red, blue, and green wool.
Two panels joined; 88" long x 81" wide.

Coverlet 50

Coverlet 50 (reverse)
Weaver: Unidentified.
Origin: Unidentified.
Inscrip: LIBERTY
Structure: tied-beiderwand
Warp: natural and blue botton. Weft: natural cotton and blue wool.
Two panels joined; 88" long x 78" wide.

Coverlet 51
The eagle trademark in Harry Tyler's later coverlets replaced the earlier lions (Coverlets 29, 41, & 42). They are done in several variations and with some turned sideways. It is said that his son Elman designed them, as he wanted something more American. In another example of Tyler's versatility, even the design of the fences varies.

Coverlet 51 (reverse)
Weaver: Harry Tyler.
Origin: Butterville, Jefferson Co., New York.
Client: Mary Ann Shutleff
Inscrip: MARY.ANN.SHUTLEFF/JEFFERSON.CO.N.Y./1845
Structure: double weave
Warp: natural cotton and strawberry red wool. Weft: natural cotton and strawberry red wool.
Two panels joined; 88" long x 83" wide.

Coverlet 52
John B. Welty died in December of 1841. Coverlets woven after that date until approximately 1854 are likely to have been woven by his widow Catharine or an associate, George Oertel.[3] The corner block inscription, however, remained unchanged.

Coverlet 52 (reverse)
Weaver: John B. Welty.
Origin: Boonsboro, Washington Co., Maryland.
Inscrip: JOHN.B./WELTY./BOONSBORO/WASHINGT./ON.COUNTY./MARYLAND/.1845.
Structure: tied-beiderwand
Warp: natural and blue cotton. Weft: natural cotton and red, and light and dark blue wool.
Two panels joined; 94" long x 84" wide.

Coverlet 53
The delightful train motif in this coverlet is unquestionably celebrating railroading as an industry and was made in Hempfield Township, Pennsylvania. However, it cannot be specifically honoring the well-known Hempfield Railroad, since the coverlet was made several years before that railroad was constructed. Compare this with Coverlets 87 & 88.

Coverlet 53 (reverse)
Weaver: Jacob Lutz.
Origin: East Hempfield Township, Lancaster Co., Pennsylvania.
Client: Sarah Heidelbau
Inscrip: MADE BY/J. LUTZ.HEMPFIELD/TOWNSHIP./FOR/SARAH/HEIDELBAU/1848.
Structure: tied-beiderwand
Warp: natural cotton. Weft: natural cotton and brick red, scarlet red, blue, and celery green wool.
Two panels joined; 87" wide x 81" long.

Coverlet 54
The client's name appears under only one of the trademark corner blocks and is readable only on the dark side at right. Notice the variations of the top and bottom borders.

Coverlet 54 (reverse)
Weaver: Asahel Amora Phelps.
Origin: Delhi, Delaware Co., New York.
Client: Jane Schermerhorn
Inscrip: DELHI.1846./JANE./SCHERMERHORN
Structure: double weave
Warp: natural cotton and brick red wool. Weft: natural cotton and brick red wool.
Two panels joined; 104” long x 80” wide.

Coverlet 55

Coverlet 55 (reverse)
Weaver: J. Shafer (full name unknown).
Origin: Martinsburg, Blair Co., Pennsylvania.
Client: Catharine Greser
Inscrip: CATHA/RINE/GRESER/1846/J.SHAFER/MARTINS/BURG/BLAIR/CO.PA
Warp: natural and brown cotton. Weft: natural cotton and red, blue, and green wool.
Two panels joined; 88” long x 77” wide.

Coverlet 56
The origin of this coverlet is unidentified, although Mildred Davison places it in Ohio.[4] Indeed, the colors, structure, and general look and feel of the pattern most strongly suggest Ohio, perhaps the Western Reserve area. Aspects of the pattern execution seem almost primitive, but the effect is strong and bold. The warm combination of the colors (and the placement of the red) makes this a personal favorite.

Coverlet 56 (reverse)
Weaver: Unidentified.
Origin: Unidentified.
Inscrip: GEN.WASHINGTON/LIBERTY
Structure: double weave
Warp: natural cotton and red and blue wool. Weft: natural cotton and red and blue wool.
One panel, seamless; 90" long x 78" wide.

Coverlet 57
Field pattern motifs turned 90 degrees like this are unusual.

Coverlet 57 (reverse)
Weaver: Unidentified.
Origin: Unidentified.
Inscrip: CAPITOL IN WASHINGTON/1846
Structure: double weave
Warp: natural cotton and blue wool. Weft: natural cotton and blue wool
Two panels joined; 89" long x 80" wide.

Coverlet 58
Compare this with Coverlet 59, also by Fasig. It is hard to believe the same weaver made two such different coverlets!

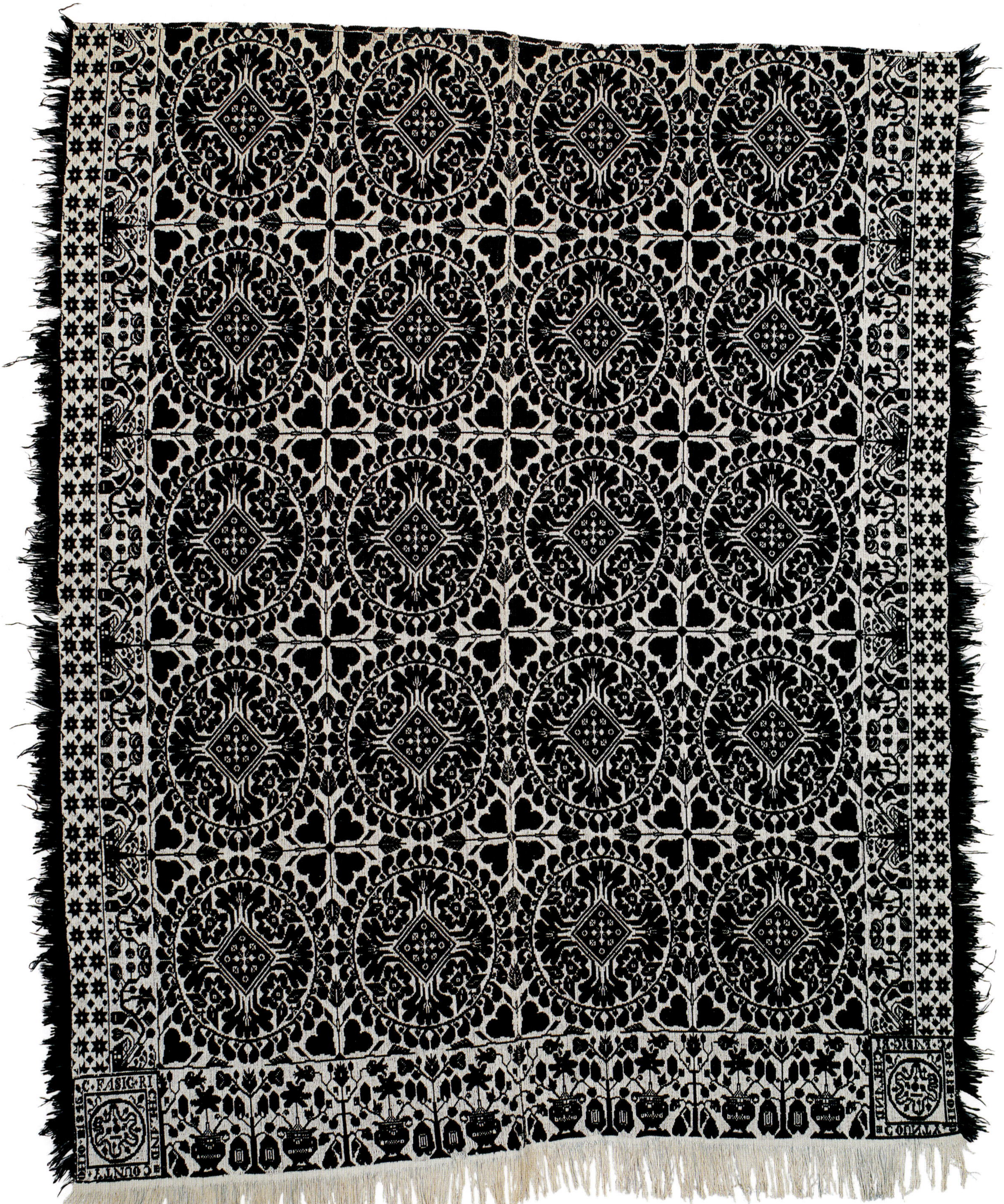

Coverlet 58 (reverse)
Weaver: Christian Fasig.
Origin: Richland Co., Ohio.
Inscrip: C.FASIG.RI/CH.LAND./COUNTY./OHIO.1846
Structure: tied-beiderwand
Warp: natural and blue cotton. Weft: natural cotton and blue wool.
Two panels joined; 82" long x 71" wide.

Coverlet 59
The execution of this coverlet seems much more refined than the previous one and perhaps signifies the acquisition of better equipment. Mr. Fasig has, in this later example, also redesigned his trademark corner block. He had to abbreviate his first and last names and the word "Ohio" in order to squeeze in his inscription.

Coverlet 59 (reverse)
Weaver: Christian Fasig.
Origin: Richland Co., Ohio.
Inscrip: CHRISTIA/FAS.G./RIC/HLAND.CO/UNTY/OHI/1847
Structure: tied-beiderwand
Warp: natural and brown cotton. Weft: natural cotton and blue wool.
Two panels joined; 84" long x 71" wide.

Coverlet 60

Coverlet 60 (reverse)
Weaver: Carl Lewis Kean.
Origin: Louisville, Jefferson Co., Kentucky.
Inscrip: MADE.BY./C.L.KEAN.
Structure: tied-beiderwand
Warp: natural and blue cotton. Weft: natural cotton and blue wool.
Two panels joined; 97" wide x 98" long.

Coverlet 61

Coverlet 61 (reverse)
Weaver: Unidentified.
Origin: Pennsylvania (attrib).
Client: Nancy Hixson
Inscrip: NANCY/HIXSON/1847
Structure: tied-beiderwand
Warp: natural cotton. Weft: natural cotton and blue wool.
Two panels joined; 95” long x 67” wide.

Coverlet 62
The carpet-like arrangement of florals and bars is reminiscent of Balantyne's Scottish heritage. Many British weavers made ingrain carpets as well as coverlets.

Coverlet 62 (reverse)
Weaver: Samuel Balantyne.
Origin: Lafayette, Tippecanoe Co., Indiana.
Inscrip: S./BALANTYNE/1847.
Structure: double weave
Warp: natural cotton and blue wool. Weft: natural cotton and blue wool.
Two panels joined; 91" long x 77"wide.

Coverlet 63
There were several Craigs in Indiana, including William, Sr., William, Jr., and James (father and sons) from Decatur County, and James of Washington County. Corner blocks of the Craig coverlets are all-important in determining who made any particular one. The lily and the date of 1848 tell us this example was by James Craig of Decatur County, in his early days.

Coverlet 63 (reverse)
Weaver: James Craig.
Origin: Decatur County, Indiana.
Inscrip: 1848
Structure: double weave
Warp: natural cotton and blue wool. Weft: natural cotton and blue wool.
Two panels joined; 91" long by 74" wide.

Coverlet 64
The corner block here is the well-known courthouse motif, with the date. It signifies that William, Sr., James, or William, Jr., could have made this coverlet. (James of Washington County also used the courthouse but did not date his coverlets.) The eagles and the LIBERTY inscriptions in the field are very subtle here.

Coverlet 64 (reverse)
Weaver: Craig Family.
Origin: Decatur County, Indiana.
Inscrip: 1848/LIBERTY
Structure: double weave
Warp: natural cotton and blue wool. Weft: natural cotton and blue weft.
Two panels joined; 87" long x 77" wide.

Coverlet 65
The neo-classical houses with their picket fences and adjoining trees seem unique to Shamp. The composition of the circular foliate motifs of the field (surrounding the large stars), work nicely with the trees in the border.

Coverlet 65 (reverse)
Weaver: D. Shamp (attrib.).
Origin: Darien, Genesee County, New York.
Inscrip: 1849/DARIEN.GENESEE CO.N.Y.
Structure: double weave
Warp: natural cotton and pink wool. Weft: natural cotton and pink wool.
Two panels joined; 89” long x 72” wide.

Coverlet 66
The quilt-like arrangement of the pattern blocks and the letters "A" through "L" makes one wish for a "sister" coverlet with the rest of the letters. Alas, none is known to exist. M. Krady could be either the customer or the weaver.

Coverlet 66 (reverse)
Weaver: M. Krady (weaver or client ?).
Origin: Pennsylvania (attrib.)
Inscrip: 1849/ABCDEFG/HIJKL
Structure: tied-beiderwand
Warp: natural and blue cotton. Weft: natural cotton the red, blue, and green wool.
Two panels joined; 98" long x 92" wide.

Coverlet 67
This coverlet, from the Western Reserve area of Ohio, suggests a nice day in the country. The two dogs are chasing a fox, and birds and butterflies are flying in their respective field. The spotted dog is an almost exact likeness of one of Thomas Bewick's woodcuts. The butterflies might actually be silk moths, as Ohio was active in the silk industry at this time (*see Animals, pg. 10*). This coverlet dates to about 1848 when McLeran is known to have been in Salem.

Coverlet 67 (reverse)
Weaver: James McLeran.
Origin: Salem, Columbiana Co., Ohio.
Inscrip: J.McLERAN/SALEM/OHIO
Structure: double weave
Warp: natural cotton and red and blue wool. Weft: natural cotton and red and blue wool.
Two panels joined; 87" long x 79" wide.

Coverlet 68
The Muir Family included Robert, Thomas, John, and William; and all used the same trademark. It is not known which brother wove this piece.

Coverlet 68 (reverse)
Weaver: Muir Family.
Origin: Wayne, Greencastle, and Putnam Counties, Indiana.
Inscrip: 1849
Structure: double weave
Warp: natural cotton and blue wool. Weft: natural cotton and blue wool.
Two panels joined; 97" long x 83" wide.

Coverlet 69

Coverlet 69 (reverse)
Weaver: John Long.
Origin: (town unknown), Holmes Co., Ohio
Inscrip: JOHN.LONG/HOLMES/COUNTY/OHIO/1850/SP
Structure: tied-beiderwand
Warp: natural cotton. Weft: natural cotton and red and blue wool.
Two panels joined; 80" long x 71" wide.

Coverlet 70
Notice the side border with the tiny farmer, his cow, and his little farmhouse, with tiny birds in flight. The bottom border depicts leafless trees, menorahs, and cornucopias. This is very different from the work of his brother James (Coverlet 63).

Coverlet 70 (reverse)
Weaver: William Craig Jr.
Origin: Greensburg, Decatur Co., Indiana
Inscrip: W.CRAIG/GREENSBURG/DC.CO.IA/1850
Structure: double weave
Warp: natural cotton and blue wool. Weft: natural cotton and blue weft.
Two panels joined; 89" long x 70" wide.

Coverlet 71

Rossville is on Staten Island, New York, site of an early Dutch settlement; and the tied-beiderwand structure of this piece would be consistent with that heritage. The weaver's trademark corner block bears a strong likeness to the Royal Crest of Holland. The various villages and towns in that country replaced the center of the design with their own unique ones; and this weaver has chosen to use his initials there, surrounded by a laurel wreath. The number "51" cannot be the number of the coverlet, as at least one other with the same number is extant. It could be the date, but 1851 is very late for handspun materials such as these to appear in an east-coast location, long after mill-run yarns were readily available there. Perhaps it is the weaver's age when he wove it. Notice the abbreviation WER, probably for the word "weaver" – the "W" would have been pronounced as a "V."

Coverlet 71 (reverse)
Weaver: IFC (full name unknown).
Origin: Rossville, Richmond Co., New York.
Inscrip: IFC/ROSSVILLE.51./COVERLET.WER
Structure: tied-beiderwand
Warp: natural cotton. Weft: natural cotton and blue wool.
Two panels joined; 93" long x 72" wide.

Coverlet 72
A man's name on a coverlet is not always that of the weaver, as one can see here.

Coverlet 72 (reverse)
Weaver: Jacob Witmer.
Origin: Manor Township, Lancaster Co., Pennsylvania
Client: Jacob Habecker
Inscrip: MADE BY/J.WITMER/MANOR/TOWNSHIP/FOR/JACOB/HABECKER/1851
Structure: tied-beiderwand
Warp: natural cotton. Weft: natural cotton and blue wool.
Two panels joined; 103” long x 87” wide.

Coverlet 73

Coverlet 73
Weaver: Unidentified.
Origin: Unidentified.
Client: Rosana H. Winger
Inscrip: ROSANA/H./WINGER/1851
Structure: tied-beiderwand
Warp: natural cotton. Weft: natural cotton and blue wool.
Two panels joined; 85" long x 65" wide.

Coverlet 74

Coverlet 74
Weaver: Henry Miller.
Origin: McCutchenville, Seneca Co., Ohio
Inscrip: HENRY./MILLER./McCUTCHEN/VILLE./SENECA./.OHIO./1851
Structure: tied-beiderwand
Warp: natural and blue cotton. Weft: natural cotton and blue wool.
Two panels joined; 89” long x 68” wide.

Coverlet 75
The fiery composition of the starbursts and floral tiles make one think of a stained glass window in a church. The "church" is landscaped with a happy border of potted, stylized flowers. The Seifert & Co. trademark corner block, with its large public building and its detailed inscription, proudly advertise their work. "SUPERIOUR" is a rather florid spelling in its own right! Although this coverlet is undated, it is known that the three Seifert brothers worked together from approximately 1843 to 1851.

Coverlet 75 (reverse)
Weaver: Seifert & Co.
Origin: Mechanicsburg, Cumberland Co., Pennsylvania
Inscrip: SUPERIOUR.COVERLETS./MANUFACTURED.THE.LATEST.FASHION.BY.SEIFERT.&CO./ MECHANICS/BURG.CUMBERLAND.COUNTY./PENNSYLVANIA.
Structure: tied-beiderwand
Warp: natural and blue cotton. Weft: natural cotton and red, blue, and green wool.
One panel, seamless; 101" long x 98" wide.

Coverlet 76
Unexpected as they are, exotic animals appear occasionally on coverlets. Perhaps they were inspired by a drawing in a book or by a travelling show. This was an era of great discoveries and interest in things new and different, especially animals (*see Animals, pg. 10*).

Coverlet 76 (reverse)
Weaver: HR (weaver or client?).
Origin: Unidentified.
Inscrip: 1852./H.R.
Structure: double weave
Warp: natural cotton and red and blue wool. Weft: natural cotton and red and blue wool.
Two panels joined; 88" long x 81" wide.

Coverlet 77
Musselman was a prolific weaver who numbered his coverlets. This one is "No. 879." He dropped one "L" from the word Hilltown, reduced the size of one "T," and didn't have room for the entire state of "Pennsylvania." Nevertheless, he got the message across with this nice work. Compare this with his later coverlet (Coverlet 95).

Coverlet 77 (reverse)
Weaver: Samuel B. Musselman.
Origin: Hilltown, Bucks Co., Pennsylvania
Client: Isaac Kolb
Inscrip: S.B.MUS/SELMAN/COVERLET/WEAVER/HILTOWN/BUCKS.CO/NO 879/.THIS./COVERLET/BELONGS/TO/ISAAC/KOLB/.1853.
Structure: tied-beiderwand
Warp: natural and blue cotton. Weft: natural cotton and red, blue, and ochre wool.
One panel, seamless; 101" long x 77" wide.

Coverlet 78
The unusual crest on the side border appears to be a European-influenced design with its crown and sheep. Its significance to the weaver is, alas, unknown, although it presumably relates to his heritage. The materials are handspun.

Coverlet 78 (reverse)
Weaver: I.G. (full name unknown).
Origin: Unidentified
Inscrip: IG.
Structure: tied-beiderwand
Warp: natural and blue cotton. Weft: natural cotton and red and blue wool.
Two panels joined; 89" long x 70" wide.

Coverlet 79
The dated courthouse trademark indicates that any of the Decatur County Craigs could have made this. The large cornucopias and elaborate floral arrangements suggest the feeling of well-being and success. "Peace and plenty" is a favorite theme in coverlets and is expressed with cornucopias, sheaves of wheat, and fruit, in many combinations. The actual inscription PEACE AND PLENTY appears on some coverlets by other weavers but is not tied to any specific pattern.

Coverlet 79 (reverse)
Weaver: Craig Family.
Origin: Decatur Co., Indiana
Inscrip: 1853
Structure: double weave
Warp: natural cotton and blue wool. Weft: natural cotton and blue wool.
Two panels joined; 88" long x 78" wide.

Coverlet 80
The birds in the bottom border are different from the usual "Birds of Paradise," and the young are not in nests. Rattray uses this motif regularly (see Coverlet 81).

Coverlet 80 (reverse)
Weaver: Matthew Rattray.
Origin: Richmond, Wayne Co., Indiana
Inscrip: 1853
Structure: double weave
Warp: natural cotton and blue wool. Weft: natural cotton and blue wool.
Two panels joined; 78" long x 79" wide.

Coverlet 81

Coverlet 81 (reverse)
Weaver: Matthew Rattray.
Origin: Richmond, Wayne Co., Indiana
Inscrip: 1853
Structure: double weave
Warp: natural cotton and red and blue wool. Weft: natural cotton and red and blue wool.
Two panels joined; 88"long x 77" wide.

Coverlet 82
The "WV," for "weaver," in this corner block is unique to William Craig, Sr. The side border, with its farmer and cow, is used by William, Jr., also; but the field pattern in this coverlet seems to belong only to William, Sr.

Coverlet 82 (reverse)
Weaver: William Craig, Sr.
Origin: Greensburg, Decatur Co., Indiana
Inscrip: W.CRAIG/WV/GREENSBURG/D.C/IA/1854
Structure: double weave
Warp: natural cotton and blue wool. Weft: natural cotton and blue wool.
Two panels joined; 92" long x 77" wide.

Coverlet 83
Note the heart in the center of each large flower in its bold tile layout. Compare with the design of the next three coverlets (Coverlets 84, 85, & 86), all made by the same weaver for different customers.

Coverlet 83 (reverse)
Weaver: Unknown.
Origin: Pennsylvania (attrib.)
Client: Maria C. Cownover
Inscrip: MARIA.C/COWNOVER
Structure: tied-beiderwand
Warp: natural and blue cotton. Weft: natural cotton and red, blue, and green wool.
Two panels joined; 94" long x 89" wide.

Coverlet 84
This coverlet features elaborate cake stands like the glass ones of the period, on top of which are stylized potted flowers. This, and the next three (Coverlets 84, 85, & 86) use the same patterns but are made for different customers. The principal differences are in shading of the green wool.

Coverlet 84 (reverse)
Weaver: Unknown.
Origin: Pennsylvania (attrib.)
Client: Elizabeth Keszler
Inscrip: ELIZABET/KESZLER
Structure: tied-beiderwand
Warp: natural and blue cotton. Weft: natural cotton and red, blue, and green wool.
Two panels joined; 96" long x 91" wide.

Coverlet 85

Coverlet 85 (reverse)
Weaver: Unknown.
Origin: Pennsylvania (attrib.)
Client: M. Roarbaugh
Inscrip: M.ROAR/BAUGH
Structure: tied-beiderwand
Warp: natural and blue cotton. Weft: natural cotton and red, blue, and green wool.
Two panels joined; 93" long x 91" wide.

Coverlet 86
The trademark corner block of this weaver is unidentified. The structure and pattern motifs used in these coverlets are similar to those of Andrew Kump of Hanover (York Co.), Pennsylvania, who sold his equipment to William Gernand in 1855. However, Gernand's corner block motifs are known. It is widely believed that Mathias Mann could be the weaver in question, but the star he uses is different.[5] The *Checklist*[6] describes a coverlet with the name Henry T. William*s* from Dover Township (York Co.), and this may be significant if it is the same man named on this coverlet. The location would be appropriate, as all these coverlets are from the same general area.

Coverlet 86 (reverse)
Weaver: Unidentified.
Origin: Pennsylvania (attrib.)
Client: Henry William (client or weaver?)
Inscrip: HENRY/WILLIAM
Structure: tied-beiderwand
Warp: natural and blue cotton. Weft: natural cotton and red, blue, and green wool.

Coverlet 87
The steam train depicted in this coverlet can be compared with the next (Coverlet 88) and with the one by Jacob Lutz (Coverlet 53). (A rod pocket has been sewn very nicely to the top of the light side of this piece.)

Coverlet 87 (reverse)
Weaver: Unidentified.
Origin: Unidentified.
Structure: double weave
Warp: natural cotton and red and blue wool. Weft: natural cotton and red and blue wool.
Two panels joined; 84" long x 80" wide.

Coverlet 88
This is the famous Hemfield Railroad coverlet, much prized by collectors. In this example, the pattern and color changes create a visual texture of a third color and a resemblance to ingrain carpeting. The correct spelling should include a "P;" but it would not have fit into the circular motif. It is not known if this is an ad hoc abbreviation brought about by space limitations, or a misspelling. After much debate and research by coverlet students, the weaver and origin of the Hemfield Railroad coverlets are still unknown.

Coverlet 88 (reverse)
Weaver: Unidentified.
Origin: Pennsylvania (attrib.)
Inscrip: HEMFIELD RAILROAD
Structure: double weave
Warp: natural cotton and salmon and blue wool. Weft: natural cotton and salmon and blue wool.
Two panels joined; 84" long x 77" wide.

Coverlet 89
The look here is more like a carpet, with its relaxed floral vine and leaf motifs.

Coverlet 89 (reverse)
Weaver: Unidentified.
Origin: Pennsylvania (attrib.)
Structure: tied-beiderwand
Warp: natural and blue cotton. Weft: natural cotton and red and light and dark blue wool.
One panel, seamless; 99" long x 92" wide.

Coverlet 90
The interesting use of blue cotton in warp and weft, creates an unusual setting for the red wool. Blue cotton used in this manner appears in Pennsylvania coverlets by other weavers as well. The corner block is at the top (head) end of the coverlet, perhaps intended to be read by the customer as he (she) was in bed. At first glance, this would appear to be an error in the placement of the attached fringe; however, several Pennsylvania makers' coverlets are done this way. The date in this corner block is virtually undecipherable but appears to be 1857.

Coverlet 90 (reverse)
Weaver: Philip Krebs.
Origin: Lebanon Co., Pennsylvania
Inscrip: KREBS/1857 (?)
Structure: tied-beiderwand
Warp: blue cotton. Weft: blue cotton and red wool.
One piece, seamless; 93" long x 81" wide.

Coverlet 91
Compare this with the next two coverlets (Coverlets 92 & 93). These pattern motifs, with many variations, have been ascribed to various weavers in Ohio and Pennsylvania.

Coverlet 91 (reverse)
Weaver: Unidentified.
Origin: Unidentified.
Structure: tied-beiderwand
Warp: natural and blue cotton. Weft: natural cotton and red, blue, and green wool.
Two panels joined; 97" long x 91" wide.

Coverlet 92
Instead of the peacocks in the side borders like the previous coverlet, this one shows potted floral arrangements.

Coverlet 92 (reverse)
Weaver: Unidentified.
Origin: Unidentified.
Structure: tied-beiderwand
Warp: natural and blue cotton. Weft: natural cotton and red wool.
Two panels joined; 96"long x 90" wide.

Coverlet 93
This coverlet utilizes smaller repeats of the peacock motif, and is done in double weave construction. This makes for a very different effect, from the previous two.

Coverlet 93 (reverse)
Weaver: Unidentified.
Origin: Unidentified.
Structure: double weave
Warp: natural cotton and red and blue wool. Weft: natural cotton and red and blue wool.
Two panels joined; 81" long x 79" wide.

Coverlet 94
Notice how the floral wreaths in the field mimic the shape of the potted flowers in the side borders. The composition here is nicely thought out!

Coverlet 94 (reverse)
Weaver: Samuel Stinger.
Origin: Carthage, Rush Co., Indiana
Inscrip: 1858
Structure: double weave
Warp: natural cotton and blue wool. Weft: natural cotton and blue wool.
Two panels joined; 88" long x 81" wide.

Coverlet 95
Unlike his earlier coverlet (Coverlet 77), Musselman has not numbered this one and does not have the inscription "PENNSYLVAN" on three sides. He is, however, still spelling "Hilltown" with only one "L."

Coverlet 95 (reverse)
Weaver: Samuel B. Musselman.
Origin: Hilltown, Bucks County, Pennsylvania
Client: Anna Funck
Inscrip: S.B./MUS/SELMAN/WEAVER/HILTOWN/BUCKS.CO/.1859 and .THIS./COVERLET/BELONGS.TO ME/ANNA/FUNCK./.1859.
Structure: tied-beiderwand
Warp: natural cotton. Weft: natural cotton and red, blue, and green wool.
One panel, seamless; 99" long x 82" wide.

Coverlet 96

Coverlet 96 (reverse)
Weaver: Unidentified.
Origin: New York (attrib.)
Inscrip: 1861
Structure: double weave
Warp: natural cotton and red wool. Weft: natural cotton and red wool.
One piece, seamless; 98" long x 88" wide.

Coverlet 97
Compare this with the next three (Coverlets 98, 99, & 100). It is amazing what a difference can be made with the use of structure, color change, and size and complexity of motif. Add a different border and the variations can seem endless. The "Birds of Paradise" theme is one of the most popular with collectors. We have long believed that one could make a first-class collection of just this one theme.

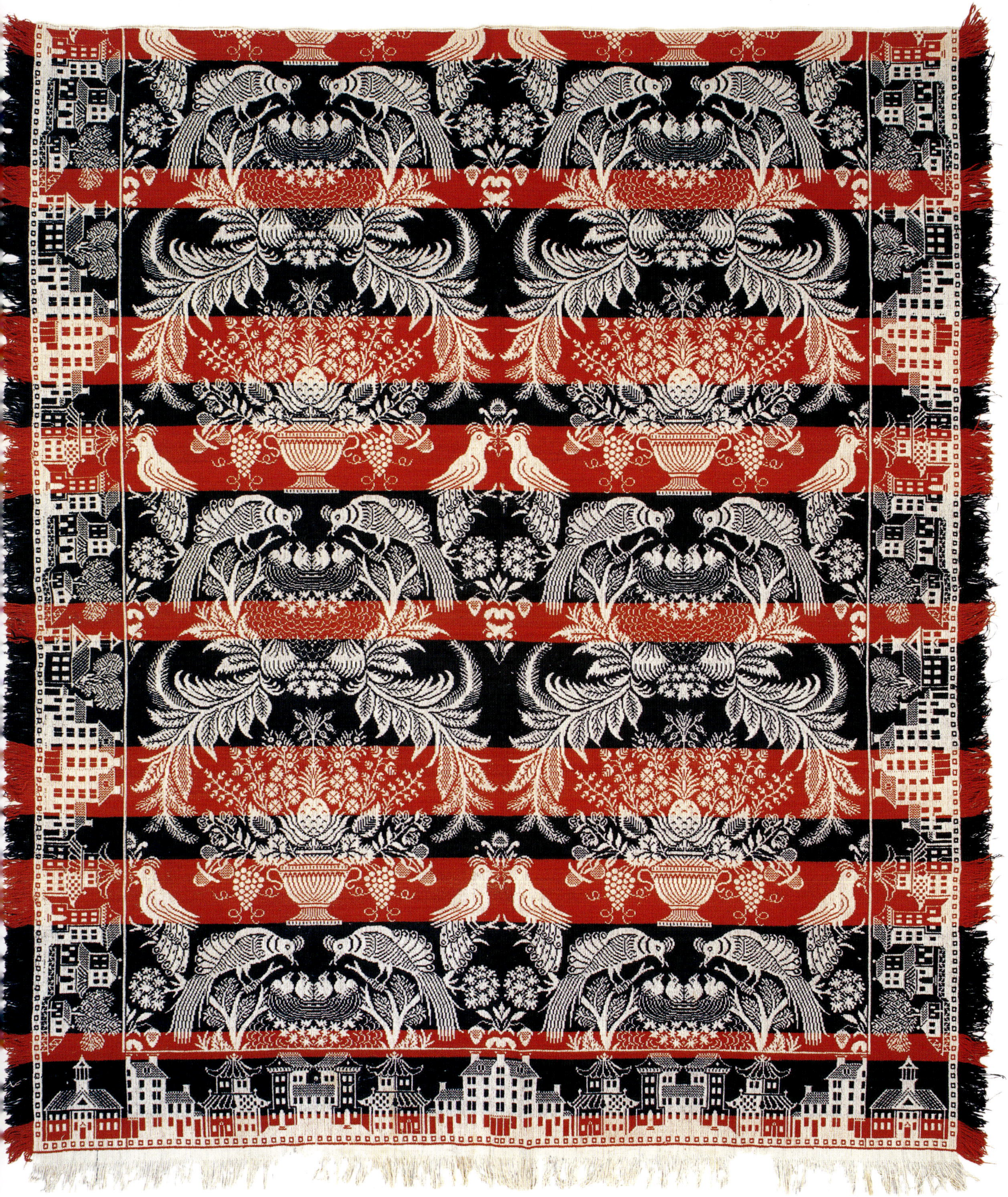

Coverlet 97 (reverse)
Weaver: Unidentified.
Origin: Unidentified.
Structure: tied-beiderwand
Warp: natural and blue cotton. Weft: natural cotton and red, and blue wool.
One piece, seamless; 89" long x 77" wide.

Coverlet 98
This example looks different from the last, partially because it is double weave instead of tied-beiderwand.

Coverlet 98 (reverse)
Weaver: Unidentified.
Origin: Unidentified.
Structure: double weave
Warp: natural cotton and red and blue wool. Weft: natural cotton and red and blue wool.
Two panels joined; 81" long x 73" wide.

Coverlet 99
This version is comparatively ornate. There are six young in the nest, rather than the usual four. The architectural border and its flags add another happy element into the mix.

Coverlet 99 (reverse)
Weaver: Unidentified.
Origin: Unidentified.
Inscrip: 1867
Structure: tied-beiderwand
Warp: natural and brown cotton. Weft: natural cotton and red and blue wool.
One panel, seamless; 85" long x 80" wide.

Coverlet 100
This coverlet is less busy than the previous one and has an interesting border of vines, which appear to spill out of flowerpots in the corners.

Coverlet 100
Weaver: Unidentified.
Origin: Unidentified.
Inscrip: MADE IN 1869
Structure: tied-beiderwand
Warp: natural cotton. Weft: natural cotton and red, blue, and green wool.
Two panels joined; 83" long x 72" wide.

Coverlet 101
This is a classic example of the patriotic theme, as seen near the end of the reign of fancy coverlets. The pattern has moved from many repeats into a large central medallion, and the piece is one seamless panel. It is virtually square. The slogan LIBERTY appears four times, surrounding four female figures. Flags fly in the center. Large eagles are perched under banners of E PLURIBUS UNUM. The classic urns and floral arrangements, together with cornucopias, surround the central motif at the borders and suggest a theme of "peace and plenty." This coverlet was made four years after the end of the Civil War (1861-1865). The choice of slogans suggests that it is celebrating the survival of the American Union.

Coverlet 101 (reverse)
Weaver: Ira Hadsell.
Origin: Palmyra, Wayne Co., New York
Inscrip: LIBERTY/E PLURIBUS UNUM/1869/WOVEN.AT.PALMYRA.N.Y.BY.IRA HADSELL
Structure: double weave
Warp: natural cotton and red wool. Weft: natural cotton and red wool.
One panel, seamless; 82" long x 80" wide.

Coverlet 102
This is an exuberant exercise in color and pattern. George Washington is surrounded by birds, horses, flags, and flowers. Almost hiding in the corners are small steamboats. Though Robert Fulton, a native of Lancaster, did not invent the steamboat, his many improvements and vast expertise in steam navigation made him an unofficial favorite son. The synthetic aniline dyes used for the colors in this coverlet are quite different in tone from the natural dyes used in earlier ones. The background texture here is common in these later pieces.

Coverlet 102 (reverse)
Weaver: Philip Schum.
Origin: Lancaster, Lancaster Co., Pennsylvania
Inscrip: WASHINGTON./HAIL 1869/MADE.BY.PHILIP.SCHUM./LANCASTER.PA
Structure: tied-beiderwand
Warp: natural and brown cotton. Weft: natural cotton and red, blue, and green wool.
One panel, seamless; 84" long x 79" wide.

Coverlet 103

Coverlet 103 (reverse)
Weaver: Unidentified.
Origin: Unidentified.
Inscrip: MEMORIAL HALL/CENTENNIAL
Structure: double weave
Warp: natural and blue cotton. Weft: natural cotton and red, light blue, medium green, and brown wool.
One panel, seamless; 78" long x 83" wide.

Coverlet 104
The Maryville Woolen Mills, located on Pistol Creek in Maryville, was in operation from 1874 to 1901. During this time it grew from three water-powered looms with about 12 employees, to 50 steam-powered looms and 60 employees.[7] The top and bottom ends of both these coverlets are machine stitched. However, the materials in both are handspun. Although the "latest improvements" were slower to reach the rural areas, handspinning was practiced much longer in the South than it was in the North, even after mill-run yarns were available. Coverlets of handspun materials were made in the Southern Highlands, as late as the 20th century.

Coverlet 104 (reverse)
Weaver: Maryville Woolen Mills.
Origin: Maryville, Blount Co., Tennessee.
Inscrip: MWM/TENN.
Structure: tied-beiderwand
Warp: natural cotton and green wool. Weft: natural cotton and green wool.
One panel, seamless; 78" long by 75" wide.

Coverlet 105

Coverlet 105 (reverse)
Weaver: Maryville Woolen Mills.
Origin: Maryville, Blount Co., Tennessee
Inscrip: MWM/TENN.
Structure: tied-beiderwand
Warp: natural cotton. Weft: natural cotton and olive-brown wool.
One panel, seamless; 82" long x 73" wide.

List of Represented Weavers

In Alphabetical Order

Alexander, James; New York - Coverlets 3 & 27
Balantyne, Samuel; Indiana - Coverlet 62
Bury, Daniel; Ohio - Coverlet 45
C., I.F. (full name unknown); New York - Coverlet 71
Christie, I. (sometimes spelled "Christy") - *see Haring, David*
Cockefair Mills; Indiana - Coverlet 40
Craig Family (James, Wm., Jr., or Wm., Sr.); Indiana – Coverlets 64 & 79
Craig, James (Decatur Co.); Indiana - Coverlet 63
Craig, William Jr.; Indiana - Coverlet 70
Craig, William Sr.; Indiana - Coverlet 82
Cunningham, James; New York, Coverlets 35 & 36
Davidson, Archibald; New York, Coverlets 11 & 21
Denholm, John; Pennsylvania - Coverlet 34
Fasig, Christian; Pennsylvania - Coverlets 58 & 59
Fletcher, B. (customer or weaver?); New York - Coverlet 4
French, Bartlett; New York, Coverlet 12
G., I. (full name unknown); state unidentified - Coverlet 78
Gilmour Family (Gabriel, Joseph of Wm.); Indiana - Coverlet 32
H.R., *see R., H.*
Hadsell, Ira; New York - Coverlet 101
Haring, David D. (attr.)(or Christie); New Jersey - Coverlets 9 (*see also Coverlets 7 & 8*)
Harting, Peter (sometimes spelled "Hartung"); Pennsylvania - Coverlet 10
Hoke, Martin; Pennsylvania - Coverlets 23 & 44
I.F.C., *see C., I. F.*
I.G., *see G, I.*
Impson, Jacob; New York - Coverlets 28
Kean, Carl Lewis; Kentucky - Coverlet 60
Krady, M. (full name unknown), (customer or weaver?); Pennsylvania (attr.) - Coverlet 66
Krebs, Philip; Pennsylvania - Coverlet 90
Lamb, H. (full name unknown), (customer or weaver?); New York - Coverlet 5
Lichty, Benjamin; Ohio - Coverlet 38
Long, John; Ohio - Coverlet 69
Lutz, Jacob; Pennsylvania - Coverlet 53
McLeran, James; Ohio - Coverlet 67
Miller, Henry; Ohio - Coverlet 74
Muir Family (John, Robert, Thomas, Wm.); Indiana - Coverlet 68
Musselman, Samuel B.; Pennsylvania - Coverlets 77 & 95
MWM (Maryville Woolen Mills); Tennessee - Coverlets 104 & 105
Myer, I. (full name unknown); Pennsylvania - Coverlet 24
Oberly, Henry; Pennsylvania - Coverlet 46
Peterman, Casper; Pennsylvania - Coverlet 43
Phelps, Asahel Amora (attr.); New York - Coverlets 33 & 54
R., H. (full name unknown), (customer or weaver?); state unidentified - Coverlet 76
Rattray, Matthew; Indiana - Coverlets 80 & 81
Royer, John; Pennsylvania - Coverlet 18
Schum, Philip; Pennsylvania - Coverlet 102
Shalk, Jacob; Pennsylvania - Coverlets 16 & 17
Shafer, J. (full name unknown);Pennsylvania - Coverlet 55
Shamp, D. (full name unknown) (attr.); New York - Coverlet 65
Siefert & Co.; Pennsylvania - Coverlet 75
Smith, John; Pennsylvania - Coverlets 14, 15, & 22
Stich, G. (full name unknown); Ohio - Coverlet 39
Stringer, Samuel; Indiana - Coverlet 94
Tyler, Harry; New York - Coverlets 29, 41, 42, & 51
Van Nortwic(k), Christian; New Jersey - Coverlet 25
Welty, John B.; Maryland - Coverlet 52
William, Henry (customer or weaver?); state unidentified (PA attrib.) - Coverlet 86 (*see also Coverlets 83, 84, & 85*)
Witmer, Jacob; Pennsylvania - Coverlet 72
Young, Nathaniel (attr.); New Jersey - Coverlet 26

Unidentified Weavers

Pennsylvania – Coverlets 47, 48, 49, 50, 61, 66, & 89
New Jersey - Coverlets 2, 7, & 8
New York – Coverlets 3, 6, 13, 19, 20, 27, 30, & 96
State Unidentified - Coverlets 1, 31, 56, 57, 73, 83, 84, 85, 86 (*see William, Henry*), 87, 88, 91, 92, 93, 97, 98, 99, 100, & 103

List of Represented States

States in Alphabetical Order, Coverlets in Order of Appearance

Indiana: Coverlet 32 (Gilmour), Coverlet 40 (Cockefair Mills), Coverlet 62 (Balantyne), Coverlet 63 (Craig, James – Decatur Co.), Coverlet 64 (Craig Family), Coverlet 68 (Muir), Coverlet 70 (Craig, Wm. Jr.), Coverlet 79 (Craig Family), Coverlets 80 & 81 (Rattray), Coverlet 82 (Craig, Wm. Sr.), Coverlet 94 (Stinger)

Kentucky: Coverlet 60 (Kean)

Maryland: Coverlet 52 (Welty)

New Jersey: Coverlets 7 & 8 (Haring – attrib.), Coverlet 9 (Haring – attrib. - or Christie), Coverlet 25 (Van Nortwic(k)), Coverlet 26 (Young – attrib.)

New York: Coverlet 2 (weaver unidentified), Coverlet 3 (*see Alexander*), Coverlet 4 (Fletcher – weaver or customer?), Coverlet 5 (Lamb – weaver or customer?), Coverlet 6 (weaver unidentified), Coverlet 11 (Davidson), Coverlet 12 (French), Coverlets 13, 19 & 20 (weaver unidentified), Coverlet 21 (Davidson), Coverlet 27 (*see Alexander*), Coverlet 28 (Impson), Coverlet 29 (Tyler), Coverlet 30 (weaver unidentified), Coverlet 33 (Phelps – attrib.), Coverlets 35 & 36 (Cunningham), Coverlets 41, 42 & 51 (Tyler), Coverlet 54 (Phelps – attr.), Coverlet 65 (Shamp – attrib.), Coverlet 71 (I.F.C.), Coverlet 96 (weaver unidentified), Coverlet 101 (Hadsell)

Ohio: Coverlet 38 (Lichty), Coverlet 39 (Stich), Coverlet 45 (Bury), Coverlets 58 & 59 (Fasig), Coverlet 67 (McLeran), Coverlet 69 (Long), Coverlet 74 (Miller)

Pennsylvania: Coverlet 10 (Harting), Coverlet 14 and 15 (Smith), Coverlets 16 & 17 (Shalk), Coverlet 18 (Royer), Coverlet 22 (Smith), Coverlet 23 (Hoke), Coverlet 24 (Myer), Coverlet 34 (Denholm), Coverlet 43 (Peterman), Coverlet 44 (Hoke), Coverlet 46 (Oberly), Coverlet 47 (attrib. – weaver unidentified), Coverlet 48 (weaver unidentified), Coverlet 53 (Lutz), Coverlet 55 (Shafer), Coverlet 61 (weaver unidentified), Coverlet 66 (Krady – weaver or customer? – attr. to Pennsylvania), Coverlet 72 (Witmer), Coverlet 75 (Seifert & Co.), Coverlet 77 (Musselman), Coverlet 88 (Unidentified), Coverlet 89 (Unidentified), Coverlet 90 (Krebs), Coverlet 95 (Musselman), Coverlet 102 (Schum) – (*see also Coverlets 83, 84, 85 & 86*)

Tennessee: Coverlets 104 & 105 (Maryville Woolen Mills)

Unidentified State: Coverlets 1, 31, & 37 (weaver unidentified), Coverlets 49 & 50 (weaver unidentified), Coverlets 56, 57, 73, & 76 (weaver unidentified), Coverlet 78 (I.G.), Coverlet 83, 84, 85 & 86 (weaver unidentified – prob. Pennsylvania), Coverlets 87, 91, 92, 93, 97, 98, 99, 100 & 103 (weaver unidentified)

Endnotes

Part I

[1] Hall, Eliza Calvert. *A Book of Handwoven Coverlets*. (Little, Brown & Company: Boston, Massachusetts, 1912), p. 199.

[2] Garrett, Elisabeth Donaghy, *The Arts of Independence The DAR Museum Collection.* (The National Society, Daughters of the American Revolution; Washington, D.C., 1985), p. 21.

[3] Hall, p.279.

[4] Whisker, Vaughn E. *Tales From The Allegheny Foothills*, Volume IX. (Bedford County Press: Everett, Pennsylvania, Dec. 1, 1981), ch. 5.

[5] Hall, p. 238.

[6] Eaton, Allen H. *Handicrafts of the Southern Highlands*. (Russell Sage Foundation: New York, 1937), p. 95.

[7] *Ibid.*

[8] *Ibid.*, p. 94.

[9] *Pawtucket Sesqui-Centennial Cotton Celebration 1790-1940*. (Visitor Printing Co.: Pawtucket, Rhode Island, 1940), p. unnumbered.

[10] *Ibid.*

[11] Whisker, ch. 17.

[12] Eaton, p. 60.

[13] *Ibid.*

[14] *Ibid.*, p. 61.

[15] Hall, p. 217.

[16] *Ibid.*, p.192.

[17] *Ibid.*, p.195.

[18] *Ibid.*, p. 197.

[19] Garrett, p. 28.

[20] *Ibid.*

[21] Hall, p.192.

[22] *Ibid.*, p.186.

[23] Whisker, ch. 11.

Part II

[1] Goody, Susan Rabbit. *Woven History The Technology and Innovation of Long Island Coverlets, 1800-1860*. (Society for the Preservation of Long Island Antiquities: Setauket, Long Island,New York, 1993.) pg. 20.

[2] Anderson, Clarita S. *Weaving a Legacy The Don and Jean Stuck Coverlet Collection*. (Columbus Museum of Art: Columbus, Ohio. Distributed by Harry N. Abrams, Inc.: New York, 1995), pg. 139-140.

[3] ______. *Maryland Coverlets: The Artifacts, Technology, and the Weaver*. (University of Maryland, Ph.D. Dissertation: College Park, Maryland, 1985), pg. 321.

[4] Davison, Mildred and Christa C. Mayer-Thurman. *Coverlets A Handbook on the Collection of Woven Coverlets in the Art Institute of Chicago*. (The Art Institute of Chicago: Chicago, Illinois, 1973), pg. 159.

[5] Anderson. *Maryland Coverlets*. pg. 372.

[6] Heisey, John W., comp. *A Checklist of American Coverlet Weavers*. (The Colonial Williamsburg Foundation: Williamsburg, Virginia, 1978), pg. 117.

[7] Gammel, Paula. "History of the Maryville Woolen Mills, 1874-1901." *East Tennessee Roots, Vol. V., No. 2.* pg. 66-73.

Selected Bibliography

There are many fine references available, some of which are listed here. Most are hard to find and/or out of print, but nearly all are worth consideration for a place in the library of the serious collector. Each of these sources was used in the research and compilation of this book.

Anderson, Clarita S. *Weaving A Legacy The Don and Jean Stuck Coverlet Collection*. Columbus, Ohio: Columbus Museum of Art, Distributed by Harry N. Abrams, Inc., New York,1995.

_______. *Maryland Coverlets: The Artifacts, Technology, and the Weaver*. College Park, Maryland: Ph.D. Dissertation, University of Maryland, 1985.

Burns, Inez E. *History of Blount County Tennessee - From War Trail to Landing Strip 1795-1955*. Maryville, Tennessee: Mary Blount Chapter Daughters of the American Revolution, The Tennessee Historical Commission, 1957. Evansville, Indiana: Whipporwill Publications, 1988.

Coons, Martha, and Katherine R. Koob. *Linen-Making in New England 1640-1860*. North Andover, Massachusetts: Merrimack Valley Textile Museum, 1980.

Davison, Mildred, and Christa C. Mayer-Thurman. *Coverlets, A Handbook on the Collection of Woven Coverlets in the Art Institute of Chicago*. Chicago, Illinois: The Art Institute of Chicago, 1973.

DeGraw, Imelda G. *The Denver Art Museum Quilts and Coverlets*. Denver, Colorado: Denver Art Museum, 1974.

Eaton, Allen H. *Handicrafts of New England*. New York: Harper & Brothers, Publishers, 1949.

_______. *Handicrafts of the Southern Highlands*. New York: Russell Sage Foundation, 1937.

Gammell, Paula. "History of the Maryville Woolen Mills, 1874-1901." *East Tennessee Roots*, Vol. V., No. 2.

Garrett, Elisabeth Donaghy. *The Arts of Independence The DAR Museum Collection*. Washington, DC: The National Society, Daughters of the American Revolution, 1985.

Glick, Nancy Iona, and Katherine H. Molumby. *Illinois Jacquard Coverlets and Weavers, End of a Legacy*. Peoria, Illinois: Lakeview Museum of Arts and Sciences, 1999.

Goody, Susan Rabbit. *Woven History The Technology and Innovation of Long Island Coverlets, 1800-1860*. Setauket, Long Island, New York: Society for the Preservation of Long Island Antiquities, 1993.

Hall, Eliza Calvert. *A Book of Handwoven Coverlets*. Boston, Massachusetts: Little, Brown, and Company, 1912.

Hawthorne, Catherine B. *And So To Sleep: Jacquard Coverlets from the Hawthorne Collection*. Lowell, Massachusetts: American Textile History Museum, 1999.

_________, and Ronald L. Dotterer. *American Jacquard Coverlets*. Salisbury, Maryland: Salisbury State University, 1997.

Heisey, John W., comp. *A Checklist of American Coverlet Weavers*. Williamsburg, Virginia: The Colonial Williamsburg Foundation, 1978.

Houck, Shirley, and Robert Bitter. *The Delhi Jacquard Coverlets*. Walton, New York: The Reporter Company, Inc., 1982.

International Business Machines Corporation. *A Calculator Chronicle 300 Years of Counting and Reckoning Tools*. New York: IBM Gallery of Science and Art, undated.

Molloy, Peter M., and Laurence F. Gross. *Homespun to Factory Made: Woolen Textiles in America, 1776-1876*. North Andover, Massachusetts: Merrimack Valley Textile Museum, 1977.

Montgomery, Pauline. *Indiana Coverlet Weavers and Their Coverlets*. Indianapolis, Indiana: Hoosier Heritage Press, 1974.

Partridge, Virginia Parslow, and Rita J. Adrosko. *Made in New York State: Handwoven Coverlets 1820-1860*. Watertown, New York: Jefferson County Historical Society, 1985.

Pawtucket Sesqui-Centennial Cotton Celebration 1790-1940. Pawtucket, Rhode Island: Visitor Printing Co, 1940.

Raynor, John. *Wood Engravings by Thomas Bewick - A Selection of Engravings on Wood by Thomas Bewick*. London, New York: The King Penguin Books, Ltd., 1947.

Schorsch, Anita, ed. *Art of the Weaver*. New York: Universe Books, 1976.

Thieme, Otto C., and Joyce Marquess. *American Coverlets of the Nineteenth Century from the Helen Louis Allen Textile Collection*. Madison, Wisconsin: Elvehjem Art Center, University of Wisconsin, 1974.

Tindell, Ted. *Blount County Communities We Live In*. Maryville, Tennessee: The Brazos Press, Mrs. Marion R. Mangrum, Publisher, (undated).

Ventre, Melinda. *Warm and Wonderful The Jacquard Coverlet*. New York: Hirschl & Adler Folk, 1988.

Walker, Sandra Rambo. *Country Cloth to Coverlets - Textile Traditions in 19th Century Central Pennsylvania*. Lewisburg, Pennsylvania: Oral Traditions Project of the Union County Historical Society, 1981.

Walton, Perry. *The Story of Textiles*. New York: Tudor Publishing Co., 1925.

Wass, Janice Tauer. *Weaver's Choice, Patterns in American Coverlets*. Springfield, Illinois: Illinois State Museum, 1988.

Weissman, Judith Reiter, and Wendy Lavitt. *Labors of Love American Textiles and Needlework, 1650-1930*. New York: Alfred A. Knopf, 1987.

Whisker, Vaughn E. *Tales From The Allegheny Foothills,* Volume IX. Everett, Pennsylvania: Bedford County Press, Dec. 1, 1981.

White, Margaret E. *Hand-Woven Coverlets in the Newark Museum*. Newark, New Jersey: Newark Museum, 1947.